"This book is such a gift! I just loved this book and could not put it down! Rosen shares pragmatic advice and timeless wisdom to nurture and celebrate one's sensitive soul. Not only did I find this helpful on a personal level as a sensitive soul but it gave me new insights and compassion for those close to me who are also clearly sensitive souls. I want to buy this book in bulk and share it with everyone I know!"

— A.W.

"Christie poignantly captures the essence of the sensitive soul and offers an inspiring and compassionate perspective on how these souls inhabit our world and are simultaneously nurtured and challenged by it. She takes the reader on a graceful and often deeply personal journey through body, mind and spirit, offering daily affirmations and positive practices to help all of us—sensitive souls and lovers of sensitive souls alike—cultivate self-awareness, self-love and compassion."

—M.O.

"Christie Rosen's book explores the different ways you can center yourself: by what you consume, mindfulness, and through your relationship with others and the world around you. This book is a practical guide for anyone who feels out of balance or wants to bring more kindness and gentleness to your body, mind and soul. By creating a clear and easy personalized plan you can begin immediately, Christie's suggestions and exercises are great ways to ground yourself and actively treat yourself better. Christie's clear and concise directions and gentle approach will motivate you to treat yourself with kindness and self-care."

— C.C.

"So powerful! This is a must read for anyone looking to better understand and control their emotions. Whether you are a sensitive soul or simply someone with strong emotions who wants to better yourself and improve your mental and physical wellbeing, you will absolutely love this book. Christie combines her personal experiences as a sensitive soul with her passion for health and wellbeing to eloquently piece together a book that will undoubtedly resonate with sensitive souls and introverts alike. Along with her huge heart and desire to help others, Christie is a fabulous writer. Empowering the Sensitive Soul repeatedly invoked such strong emotions that I often felt like Christie was speaking directly to me. Each chapter left me feeling impressed with her knowledge and her ability to communicate, and fascinated as to how she got into my head and understood my problems without me having told her a thing. This is a great read written by a beautiful mind."

– B.O.

"The biggest take-away for me was that nobody needs to feel imprisoned by their sensitivities. Using the principles outlined in the book, readers will develop strategies to help affirm a more positive and powerful existence. They will learn to embrace their sensitivity and be uplifted by it. Sensitive or not, this book is a great reminder of how to live well and fully enjoy the gifts of life. As an acupuncturist, I know it will be a useful resource for my clients."

– J.B.

Empowering
the Sensitive
Soul

Simple Wisdom to Improve Your Health,
Cultivate Self-Acceptance and
Let Go of What Is Holding You Back

CHRISTIE J. ROSEN

To contact the publisher,
visit www.promotingnaturalhealth.com

To contact the author,
visit www.ChristieRosen.com

ISBN-10: 0-9982710-0-4
ISBN-13: 978-0-9982710-0-2

Library of Congress Control Number: 2016957212
Promoting Natural Health, LLC, Fort Mill, SC

Printed in the United States of America

For my mom

Table of Contents

Appendix

Welcome

"I'm sensitive. I love deeply.
I think deeply about life.
I'm honest, loyal, and true.
I appreciate the simple things.
I will not change or harden to this world.
It is this sensitivity, perception, sincerity,
awareness, affection and gentle grace
that makes me who I am."

- Lorena Page

Every soul on this earth is searching for love and acceptance. We all desire to better ourselves and live lives of meaning and purpose. As a particularly sensitive soul, you may feel that there are many obstacles in your way of living your most full, meaningful life. You may struggle to find balance and ease where others seem to excel. You may be affected by subtleties that others don't even notice. It may feel as though your strengths are not appreciated but that your perceived weaknesses are continuously called into question. It can often feel overwhelming and exhausting to even carry out a normal day. I'm here to tell you that it doesn't have to be this way and to show you how to empower yourself to live a healthy, inspired, and meaningful life.

Empowering the Sensitive Soul was born from my own journey of being a sensitive, tired, and anxious girl to becoming a vibrant, positive, and confidently sensitive woman. This book was written to help you discover, with unconditional self-acceptance, where your sensitivity is blocking you from stepping into your full potential as a human being. You will learn how to truly nurture and support yourself while also pushing yourself to let go of limiting beliefs. You will uncover your deepest areas for growth and create a personalized plan to move beyond your past and look ahead toward your bright future.

My Story

There is no question that I came into this world a sensitive soul. Whether it was being sensitive to foods, fabrics, people and smells as a baby, or being highly emotionally open and aware of other people's feelings, I have always experienced life deeply. As a little girl, I had terrible separation anxiety and still remember the great loss I felt when I had to part from my mother, even for a few hours. I wanted things a specific way. I was an incredibly picky eater. I didn't like tags on my clothes and was sensitive to laundry detergent. I was shy and felt different than my peers. I was highly sensitive.

At the age of fifteen, I started to develop chronic health issues beginning with a fluctuating thyroid condition. I felt powerless and weak. I would come home from school and sleep for hours. My heart would race uncontrollably, and for the first time in my life, I had trouble completing my school-work. I had no idea at the time that the next fifteen years of my life would be a whirlwind journey of chronic illness, self-discovery, empowerment, and healing.

Over the years, I met with countless doctors and healers for my many ailments. At various times, I was told I had thyroid disease, polycystic ovarian syndrome, interstitial cystitis, Lyme disease, anxiety, depression, adrenal fatigue, genetic mutations, multiple food sensitivities, chemical sensitivity, and more. Other times, the doctors said they could not find anything wrong with me at all! *Were they even listening to me?* It felt like the more I searched, the more the list of symptoms grew and the more confused I became. No one was helping. I was always looking for what was wrong with me and what my "fix" would be. I did not yet understand that we are multidimensional beings and there is rarely only one thing wrong or one all-encompassing fix. I also did not recognize the immense power and potential I had within myself to heal.

My first two years of college were extremely challenging for me and what I might refer to as my "rock bottom." I struggled with major sleep disruption, extreme and constant digestive upset, anxiety and depression, and was sick for weeks on end. I had a group of friends who barely knew me because I was too uncomfortable and unhappy to express myself. I did not know how to take control over my life. I was waiting for someone else to do it for me. I felt completely disempowered.

During my junior year, I had the opportunity to study abroad in Australia, which ended up being the best thing I could have done for myself at the time. I was removed from everyone I knew and got to start fresh on my own. Australia was the beginning of my fascination and experimentation with holistic health. I began practicing yoga and spent some much needed time in the sun, sand, and salt water. I went to an alternative healer and was introduced to various natural methods of healing, as well as the positive impact of a whole foods diet.

Over the next few years, my yoga practice and teaching guided me into a place of peace and strength that I had not known before. My studies at the Institute for Integrative Nutrition cemented my understanding of eating a diet rich in unprocessed natural foods, which helped me feel vibrant and free of the digestive pain I had struggled with for years. The life changing lessons I learned studying at the Institute for the Psychology of Eating helped me to truly slow down and relax into life. I intuitively knew that I was on the right path and that If I could help myself heal, I could help others do the same. As I began to share what I learned through teaching yoga and coaching clients, I felt a great sense of continuity and flow. My life and my work began to morph into my "life's work."

In my late twenties, I was busy teaching yoga and working with clients, but continued to be stuck in patterns of fatigue, anxiety, and hypersensitivity. Yoga, relaxation, and nutrition helped dramatically, but they did not feel like enough to help me break free of the issues that had been plaguing me my whole life. As I approached my thirties, I made a commitment to learn to love and accept myself exactly as I was. I decided to spend much of my twenty-ninth year focusing on bringing more self-love and positivity into my life. I had worked so much on the physical component of healing, and while that was incredibly valuable, I began to realize that now what I needed to work on most was the mental and emotional components.

It was not until I learned to let go of my limiting thought patterns and to look at myself with unconditional love and support that I was truly able to heal. I learned to see that my sensitivity is my finest gift and my biggest teacher, not something that needs to hold me back. I now feel powerful and free in a way I hadn't thought possible, and so much of that has to do with deciding to take control over my life.

This book is a direct reflection of my personal journey, and it is my hope that you will use this book to help you grow and heal on your own journey. I can promise you that if you are willing and ready for the challenge, a more positive, healthy, empowered, and full life is yours for the taking.

Are You a Sensitive Soul?

Do you consider yourself a sensitive soul? Anyone who resonates with the term is welcome to consider him or herself a sensitive soul, but you may feel particularly sensitive and vulnerable to this loud, busy, and often intimidating world.

1. Are you easily affected by the energy or moods of others?
2. Are you sensitive to criticism?
3. Do you have strong emotions?
4. Do you struggle to maintain balance and positivity in your life?
5. Do need more time to rest than you think is normal?
6. Do you have trouble managing stress?
7. Do your friends and family comment that you are overly sensitive?
8. Are you sensitive to particular foods, chemicals, fabrics, bright lights and/or smells?

If this sounds like you, you are definitely a sensitive soul and I look forward to taking this journey with you. Even if this does not sound like you, but you consider yourself a sensitive soul or love someone who is a sensitive soul, I welcome you equally to enjoy and learn from the teachings in this book. The simple yet timeless wisdom provided can truly be applied to anyone who is interested in improving their health and wellbeing, sensitive soul or not.

If you are unclear if you are sensitive and would like to

access yourself further, I recommend Dr. Elaine Aron's test, "Are you Highly Sensitive?" found on her website: hsperson. com. Dr. Aron has written multiple books on sensitive people, most notably, *The Highly Sensitive Person*, which I recommend as a great supplement to *Empowering the Sensitive Soul.* In her research she has found that approximately 15-20 percent of the population is highly sensitive.

Whether or not you qualify as a "Highly Sensitive Person" on Dr. Aron's test, if you feel sensitive or that you have sensitivities, you are welcome to consider yourself a sensitive soul. In my experience, a "sensitive person" has too often been associated with a negative connotation. I aim to feel empowered by my sensitivity, which is what being a sensitive soul does for me. Choose any title for yourself that you feel uplifted or empowered by, or perhaps choose not to use one at all. What matters most is not how you choose to define yourself, but rather the personal insights you can gain from understanding sensitivity.

The Path of Empowerment

My mission for this book is to guide you on your path of self-acceptance and healing so that you can live a full life and share your unique gifts with the world. For easy reading, this book is broken down into three major sections: *Body, Heart, and Mind.* Each offers simple yet powerful actions to take to improve your wellbeing. My suggestion is that you read the book once through and then go back to the areas that you need to work on most. Each topic discussed is short and sweet so you can come back to the book anytime you need inspiration or guidance. You can also choose to go at your own pace and take it one section at a time.

If at any point while reading you become overwhelmed with the suggestions, put the book down, take a deep breath, and check in with what you need in that moment. You may need to stop and focus on just one topic, to journal about how you are feeling, or simply take a break from the book and come back to it again later. Give yourself permission to use the book in any way that serves you best.

The *Body* section will cover the power of eating whole foods, how stress affects your digestive system, and the importance of meal timing and hydration. We will discuss incorporating joyful movement (my preferred term for "exercise") and healthy posture into your life, as well as the benefits of slowing down. We will discuss different relaxation and breathing techniques as well as the importance of sleep, connecting to nature, and reducing your use of chemicals. We will also talk about exploring different healing modalities.

The *Heart* section focuses on the importance of self-love and compassion as well as learning to trust yourself. We will talk about the importance of expressing your feelings, prioritizing yourself, appreciation, and accepting criticism. We will also discuss eliminating negative comparison, practicing forgiveness, protecting your energy, and the value of opening your loving heart. You will also brainstorm ways to find more balance in your life.

The *Mind* section focuses on the invaluable tools of choosing a positive outlook, accepting what is, choosing your words with care, and responding rather than reacting. We will work toward letting go of limiting beliefs, practicing visualization, being present in the moment, and becoming more open-minded. We will also discuss organization, the power of letting go of the little things, and releasing perfectionism.

Each topic of the book will begin with a positive affirmation. Affirmations are simple yet deeply effective in the comprehensive healing process. You will use affirmations to take power back into your hands by choosing to think empowering, life-affirming, and therapeutic thoughts. While you cannot choose every thought you have, you do have more ability to direct your mind towards empowering thoughts than you may realize.

Did you know that you think practically the exact same thoughts every day as you go about your daily routine? This is because the brain always wants to take the path of least resistance and the more frequently you think a thought, the deeper a pathway in the brain is constructed to help you think that thought again and again. You can relate thinking a common thought to walking through a snowy field with a path that has been walked through many times before. It feels easy and natural, whereas thinking a totally new thought is like walking through that same snowy field for the first time, requiring a new mindset to be established (and practiced) to make that new thought ultimately come with little effort. The more you walk through a particular path, the easier it becomes, so the more you think a certain thought, the easier it is to think it again.

Using affirmations can help you expedite and reinforce the empowerment process. I recommend repeating each affirmation provided out loud as you read the book to see how they feel to you. If you feel uplifted and empowered, that is an excellent sign to continue to use that affirmation. If it feels forced or fake, it is better to skip it and use one that you connect to. Repeating something that you have too much resistance to can actually bring up feelings of insecurity and unworthiness. You may not be ready for each affirmation at this time. Know that you can always come back to them in the future. Also, keep in mind that they are meant to help you out of patterns of negative thinking so it is okay if you don't fully believe them yet. In time, you will. You just have to be open to it.

Once you decide which affirmations resonate with you, you can create an affirmation ritual. I recommend repeating your affirmation(s) at least ten times in the morning and ten times in the evening, as well as other times throughout the day when you remember. Eventually, the beneficial affirmation will come naturally, replacing the old negative thoughts. These affirmations will then become part of who you are and how you identify yourself.

In addition to the affirmations, each topic will include key practice steps for you to follow. The practice steps not only guide you to improve in that area, but they also serve as a summary of that topic so you can look back on it easily.

After the practice steps, there may be an optional question to answer regarding the topic. You will also find space to write a personal goal you have for that area, if you feel inspired to do so. Please approach this in any way that is helpful to your personal journey.

There are a lot of suggestions and practice steps in the book, so the last section, *Your Transformation*, will help you discover where to start. You will have time to access each topic and create goals to move forward in the areas you want to work on most. You will also create specific affirmations for your goals, write a commitment letter to yourself, and envision your future. Please set time aside to do these exercises as they are incredibly impactful.

Major change takes both time and commitment to your goals. It is not going to happen overnight, but once it is set in motion, like a ripple effect, every area of your life will begin to shift. A willingness to change is the crucial first step.

I am so excited that you are on this journey with me, and I trust that you are reading this book at this time because you are ready to grow and evolve. Let's begin the journey of empowering your sensitive soul by learning to nurture your body, heart and mind, clarifying your goals, and letting go of what is holding you back.

To empowering your sensitive soul,

Christie J. Rosen

PART 1

Body

Affirmation:
*"I honor and protect my body,
no matter what."*

Nurturing and supporting your body is one of the most fundamental practices you can do. We tend to take our bodies for granted. We regularly push them too hard, feed them unhealthy foods, and criticize them for not looking the way we want them to. Regardless of how you treat your body, it will always continue to work toward healing. It is what the body is designed to do. Learning to help your body by providing it with the right conditions for healing will completely transform your life. Through healthy eating, joyful movement, adequate relaxation and more, you can learn to work with your sensitive body rather than against it, to be strong and healthy. Let's get started.

1

Healing Whole Foods

Affirmation:
*"I lovingly nourish my body with
healing whole foods."*

It can be quite challenging to know what to eat. Heavily processed "food-like" products unfortunately dominate our food supply, and you cannot pick up a magazine or browse the internet without stumbling across contradictory nutrition advice. Are you supposed to eat low fat or high fat? Vegan or paleo? Raw or all-cooked? There are so many diets out there that it is impossible to even keep track of them all. Our ancestors must have known how to eat, otherwise we wouldn't be here, so why is it so difficult for us?

Eating became quite complicated in the mid-twentieth century with the increased production of processed foods and the advent of fast food restaurants. With this, nutritional efficacy was sacrificed in exchange for ease and convenience, and the modern food industry was born. To increase profit, the food industry wanted their food to not only taste great but to also be shelf-stable and to look appealing. For these reasons, additives like chemicals, dyes, sweeteners, oils, and salts were introduced into common foods. "Food-like" products were created, containing proteins and chemical compounds significantly altered from their original state, which humans have not evolved to safely digest. Over the years, and with thanks to the massively influential marketing engines of companies like Monsanto, Americans became more and more accustomed to eating these processed foods until they ultimately became commonplace. Then, we started to get sick.

Due to the increasing prevalence of cancer, heart disease, diabetes, and obesity, we are finally at a breaking point where the damage this processed food diet has on our health can no longer be ignored. Luckily, there is a simple way of eating that is very intuitive. As the well-known food writer, Michael Pollen, would say, "Eat real food, not too much, mostly plants." The majority of the food you eat should be "whole" or "real," meaning as close to nature as possible. For example, an apple is a whole food, but Apple Jacks cereal is not. When in doubt, ask yourself where the food was before it arrived at the market. Was it **created** in a factory or **grown** on a farm? Would your ancestors recognize it as food? If not, go for something else. Learn to be mindful of what you ingest.

In addition to consuming whole foods, a healthy diet needs to include a nutritious balance of the three macronutrients: protein, fat, and carbohydrates. These are the most important nutrients that the human body needs to maintain good health. (Water is also technically a macronutrient, but we will get to that in a later section.) This balance isn't something you need to specifically calculate, but you do want to make sure you are getting high quality protein, fat, and carbohydrates daily, preferably each at every meal. It is important to consume carbohydrates in the form of vegetables, especially making sure to eat plenty of dark leafy green vegetables such as kale, collard greens, and arugula. In moderation, fruit, beans, and whole grains can also be healthy sources of carbohydrates. It is rare that someone struggles with a lack of carbohydrates in their diet, but quite common to not be getting enough healthy ones.

Your diet should also be rich in healthy fats such as coconut oil, olive oil, avocado, nuts, and seeds. If you have a fear of fat, it is time to let it go because high quality fat is essential to the human body. Limiting fat can create all kinds of unwanted conditions such as poor digestion, an inability to lose weight, fatigue, irritability, constant hunger, and more.

You also need adequate protein in your diet either from grass-fed or free-range meat and poultry, wild caught fish, free-range eggs, or legumes, nuts, and seeds. If your protein is too low, you can develop conditions such as fatigue, muscle pain, headaches, binge eating, dry skin and nails, and an inability to lose weight.

Macronutrient Overview

Healthy Carbohydrates:
- Vegetables, especially dark leafy greens
- Whole grains
- Beans and lentils
- Fruit

Healthy Fat:
- High quality oils, such as coconut oil and extra virgin olive oil
- Avocado
- Nuts and seeds
- Wild caught fish
- Free-range or pastured eggs
- Nut butters

Healthy Protein:

- Grass-fed/free-range meat and poultry
- Wild caught fish
- Free-range or pastured eggs
- Nuts and seeds
- Nut butters
- Beans and lentils
- Seaweed

In order to get the best quality nutrition, it is also crucial to choose organic, local, and non-GMO food whenever possible. Organic farming is not just beneficial for humans, but for animals, plants, and the environment as a whole. Preservation of natural resources is a key component of organic farming, and synthetic materials such as antibiotics, pesticides, added hormones, and unnecessary chemicals that are foreign to the human body are avoided. Organic farmers have specific guidelines to uphold and undergo annual inspections to maintain certification. Some small local farms are not certified organic, but may actually have just as good quality crops because getting the organic seal can often be costly and difficult to acquire. The best thing to do is go right to the farmer or farmer's market and ask how they run their farm. Those who care strongly for our environment and believe in the importance of eating the best quality food possible will be happy to share their practices with you. Keep in mind that what we are calling "organic" is not some special new age thing. It is what humans have been eating since the dawn of time. "Conventionally" grown food is what is new, unnatural, and dangerous to humans, especially long term.

If buying all organic is not feasible financially, start with buying organic animal products, as conventional animal products often contain unwanted hormones and/or antibiotics. Another money saving tips is to eat smaller portions of meat. This will be a healthy choice for your body and your wallet.

It is also important to buy organic produce where you eat the skin, such as strawberries, celery, apples, peaches, and grapes. The skin of conventional produce is where most of the toxic pesticides and chemicals reside. The Environmental Working Group creates a list every year of the "dirty dozen" (the twelve produce items found to contain the highest pesticide level) and the "clean fifteen" (the fifteen produce items tested with the lowest pesticide level). This list can help you determine the produce that is most important to buy organic.

2016 Dirty Dozen

1. Strawberries

2. Apples

3. Nectarines

4. Peaches

5. Celery

6. Grapes

7. Cherries

8. Spinach

9. Tomatoes

10. Sweet bell peppers
11. Cherry tomatoes
12. Cucumbers

2016 Clean Fifteen

1. Avocados
2. Sweet corn*
3. Pineapples
4. Cabbage
5. Frozen sweet peas
6. Onions
7. Asparagus
8. Mangoes
9. Papayas*
10. Kiwis
11. Eggplant
12. Honeydew melon
13. Grapefruit
14. Cantaloupe
15. Cauliflower

*Please note that some sweet corn and papaya may be genetically modified. To be safe, buy the organic varieties.

Keep in mind that each time you buy something, you are casting a vote for that product. If we all consistently buy organic products, the companies and farmers will be forced to supply our demand. It is also helpful to realize that good quality food is your real health insurance. You can choose to pay the farmer now or the doctor later.

Another benefit of this minimally processed, organic diet is that you will not have to watch your calories or read labels because you will know what you are eating is wholesome and nutrient dense. The saying is true—you literally are what you eat. When you feed your body real natural food, your body will respond accordingly by becoming more natural, healthy, and whole all by itself.

As a sensitive soul, you may be sensitive to particular foods. I was always a picky eater, but it wasn't until I was a teenager that I first identified my true sensitivity to food. My mom and I would frequently go to the local diner for pancakes on Saturday mornings, which I loved, but I could not understand why after eating the delicious pancakes (with fake maple syrup) I would soon become overwhelmingly lethargic. I felt like I could hardly make the thirty-second walk back to the car, let alone do anything afterward. I knew something was causing me to feel this way, but it took me a year before coming to realize that I was being severely affected by sugar, especially when eaten in the morning.

It seemed like everyone else could eat pancakes or sugary cereal and go about their day feeling fine. *Why was I different?* It wasn't long before I started to take notice of my other food sensitivities such as dairy, gluten, soy, eggs, caffeine, alcohol, and anything artificial. For example, dairy gave me severe stomachaches, gluten made me feel tired and bloated, and even a small amount of alcohol made me feel hungover for days. Foods we think of as normal in our diet were actually doing me more harm than good! As a sensitive soul, you may likely have noticed something similar.

Do you know what foods you might be sensitive to? I recommend eliminating all processed food for a period of at least ten days (twenty-one or thirty would be even better) and then noticing how you feel. This includes also eliminating dairy, soy, gluten, processed sugar, alcohol, and caffeine. After the ten days, you can begin to reintroduce one food at a time to notice if you are sensitive to it. Each person has particular foods and ingredients that digest best for their body, and the most trusted way to find out what works for you is to try an elimination diet and see how you feel. You may be sensitive to some natural foods as well, so if you do not feel fully healthy on the elimination diet, try avoiding some of the whole foods too, especially eggs, nuts, corn, red meat and shellfish. If you would like assistance, I offer an online 10-Day Cleanse that guides you through creating a healthier diet and supports you in the process of discovering food sensitivities. Visit my website to learn more.

If you are not currently in the habit of cooking your meals, it is a good idea to start practicing. While we like to think restaurants have our health in mind, they are usually more focused on taste than health. The best way to make sure that what you are eating is healthy is to cook your food yourself. Eating at home is also the best way to know exactly what is in your food and to make sure that you are not unknowingly exposed to anything you are sensitive to. There are many healthy food blogs to choose from online and meal inspiration ideas on social media. I often follow a recipe once and then try to recreate it in my own way, as I find it more enjoyable to cook without reading directions. Like anything else, learning to cook is a process, and it takes time and patience before it becomes natural. If you aren't in the habit of cooking, give it a chance. The better you get at it, the more enjoyable it will be.

While simple in concept, eating whole foods can be quite a big challenge depending on your current diet. It is important to do the best you can, taking a realistic approach and making sure to not be too rigid or too hard on yourself. Aim to eat real food approximately ninety percent of the time. Trying to be perfect with your eating is not sustainable long-term and can lead to obsession over food, overeating, and "yo-yo" dieting (continually losing weight and gaining it back) from feeling starved. I generally recommend that my clients eat as healthy as they can during the week and then give themselves a little more flexibility on the weekends. That is what I like to do.

If you are sensitive to foods, I find it helpful to re-frame your food sensitivity as a positive quality rather than only a source of frustration. Your sensitive body is a first responder; it recognizes what is not good for it more quickly than most bodies do, which then forces you into eating healthier foods. Once you start eating healthier foods, you will feel so much better that it will become easier and more enjoyable to stick to that routine. Over time, the benefits you gain from your healthy eating will be much more profound than any fleeting gratification you may get from eating unhealthy food. I am frequently asked how I manage to eat so healthy and I always say it is actually easy because I know how badly I will feel if I eat something I am sensitive to. It is rarely worth it. Having food sensitivities has encouraged and inspired me to consistently nourish my body with healing whole foods, and for that, I am truly grateful. I believe healthy eating is the foundation to living a strong and empowered life. For what do we have if we do not have our health?

There is definitely more you can learn about healthy eating, but if you eat foods that are close to nature, monitor how you feel when you eat them and adjust accordingly, you are well on your way to eating the ideal diet for you.

Healing Whole Foods Overview

Key Practice Steps:

1. Eat whole, natural foods and choose organic and non-GMO options whenever possible.

2. Enjoy all macronutrients—protein, fat, and carbohydrates.

3. Delight in occasional treats.

Your Personal Goal: _____

_____

_____

_____

_____

_____

_____

"Let food be thy medicine and
medicine be thy food."

-Hippocrates

2
Relaxed Eating

Affirmation:
"My eating is relaxed and pleasurable."

Digestion is a very complicated and powerful process, but we often take it for granted because we feel we have no control over it. We may tend to chew our food minimally, swallow, and hope for the best. However, we have more control than we may realize. Learning to eat slowly, timing your meals properly, and relaxing around food can actually have as dramatic an effect, if not more, as what you eat because it can dramatically improve your digestion.

As a sensitive soul, you are likely to deal with digestive upset. This is not only because you may be more sensitive to foods than most, but it is also because you tend to be over-stimulated more easily. Overstimulation leads to stress in the body and the body does not digest food properly under stress.

When under stress, your sympathetic nervous system kicks in and your body expends its energy only on what is necessary to get you out of danger. Digestion slows down and can even stop completely, as it is not a necessity if you are under a real threat. There is decreased blood flow to the gut, which causes a lack of assimilation of nutrients, meaning you are not getting the benefit of what you've eaten. Conversely, when you are relaxed, your parasympathetic nervous system (also known as the relaxation response) dominates and your body knows you are safe. When in a relaxation response, your body is designed to focus on tasks that are not vital for immediate survival, but are nonetheless critical, such as healing and repair of body tissue and digestion. It is in this state that your digestive system is at its best. Metabolism and calorie burning are efficient and nutrients are assimilated properly.

Due to the nature of being highly sensitive and the busy world we live in, many sensitive souls deal with chronic low-level stress. Eating when stressed for any reason causes the body to retain fat and weight and slows the production of muscle tissue because digestion is essentially turned off. This can cause the food to sit in the stomach, leading to potential digestive upset, bloating, gas, and weight gain. When you eat while you are stressed, your metabolism actually slows down.

Even if you do not think you are particularly stressed, simply eating too fast and not chewing adequately can put the body into a stress response. Are you a fast eater? I used to be one myself. Eating too fast can occur for many reasons, such as being overly hungry, feeling anxious, a lack of attention to your food, or simply out of old habit. I frequently felt like I was suffering from all of these problems at once. I would hurriedly eat my food and then look down at the plate and wonder where it all had gone. This pattern left me feeling overly full, bloated, and frustrated with myself.

To support your digestion and overall health, learn to be a relaxed eater. Focus on the texture, taste, and smell of your food. Allow eating to be something that is done with attention and pleasure. Avoid eating while standing up, driving, running around, or doing any activity that is taking away from you being present while you eat. Instead, savor your food. You will find that when you feel pleasure from your food, you will leave the meal feeling more satisfied and you will be more in tune with when you are actually full. If you eat too fast, your body does not have time to register that it is satisfied and you will most likely either be left craving more or you will have already overeaten. Aim to eat until you feel about seventy-five percent full, and then relax. You can always go back for more if you find yourself hungry again later, but you cannot undo any food that has already been eaten.

The best way to know you are eating at a healthy, relaxed pace is to make sure you chew your food thoroughly. It can be helpful to put your fork down in between bites or to use chopsticks to help you slow down. Each bite should become as liquid-like in your mouth as possible. By chewing thoroughly, you are dramatically decreasing the work your digestive system needs to put in to pulverize your food and then deliver it in microscopic pieces to your cells for energy. Test how long it typically takes you to eat a meal, pay attention to the time, and see if you can increase the length of your meal. Trying for twenty minutes is a strong place to start. If you are always the first one in your family to finish, see if you can compete to be the slowest eater. If you suffer from acid reflux, pay special attention to the pace of your eating as eating too fast can greatly increase your risk of symptoms. The more awareness you can bring to your eating, the better.

Focusing on your breath is another helpful tool to keep you calm and relaxed during your meals. Sit up tall and take deep breaths in and out through the nose. Your body needs adequate oxygen as well as proper posture for healthy digestion. As you breathe and relax, practice appreciation for your food. This is always a great way to slow down. It is also a great idea to relax after eating by either taking a short walk or doing something you find peaceful. Lying down on your left side is also quite helpful as it places the stomach and pancreas in the best position for effective digestion.

Sensitive souls can also feel especially uneasy without a consistent meal schedule. Over the years, I have learned that if more than four or five hours has gone by and I have not had any food, I feel anxious, tired, and can't think straight. Often, I don't even feel the typical symptoms of hunger in the stomach at all. I just feel unbalanced and know it is time to eat. As a sensitive soul, you may also feel fatigue or anxiety before you feel hunger pangs. Learning to eat consistently is one of the most effective techniques for a sensitive being to feel more balanced and at ease. Without proper meal timing, that feeling of contentedness will be elusive and relaxed eating will be nearly impossible.

In my coaching practice, I see many people struggle with prioritizing a consistent meal schedule. A client recently came to me saying that she feels she eats well during the day, but cannot understand why she struggles with anxiety, fatigue, and overeating at night. When asked about her food intake during the day, she was proud to tell me that she usually skips breakfast and has only a small salad for lunch. Given her issues with overeating in the evening, I was not surprised at all to hear that she did not eat much during the day. Her overeating and imbalance in the evening is actually perfectly predictable for the daily meal schedule she had been following.

Our bodies are designed to eat in accordance with the sun. We need to "break—fast" shortly after waking up to start powering our bodies for the day. When you skip breakfast, this signals to the body that there is not food available, and the body goes into starvation mode (a stress response). Anxiety sets in because your body is telling you that something is wrong and you are in danger. Therefore, skipping meals is one of the worst things you can do for any attempt to balance your energy, mood, or to curb overeating. We eat to sustain ourselves. Food is our medicine. We have to lovingly remind ourselves that eating is an affirmation of life, not something to fear or avoid.

The first thing I had my client do was to start eating a high quality breakfast and lunch with protein. Lo and behold, after only one week of consistent meals, she had lost her desire to overeat in the evenings and was feeling much less anxious and tired. She was amazed. You simply cannot starve yourself all day and expect to feel well and eat moderately in the evening. Fighting nature never works long-term.

When planning your meal schedule, aim for a nourishing breakfast with protein within at least two hours of waking, and a hearty lunch between 12pm and 1:30pm (when the sun is at its peak). By making breakfast and lunch high priorities, you will feel strong and nourished throughout the day. Dinner is most easily digested between 5pm and 8pm.

It is also highly beneficial to avoid eating close to bedtime so that your body can focus on sleep rather than digestion. Your body's metabolism is much slower late at night and you will likely not digest your late-night food properly. Animal protein takes especially long to digest and is better eaten earlier in the day. If you eat too much too late, it will likely cause you to wake up feeling bloated and tired. I used to eat dinner very late because of my work schedule and I found that when I would eat late, I would have more trouble waking up in the morning and feel much more bloated and fatigued throughout the next day. I could feel my previous night's dinner just sitting in my stomach and it was often quite uncomfortable. Take care of yourself and plan to potentially eat less in the evenings but more throughout the day. You will feel more satisfied, have more energy, and feel more balanced in your sensitive body.

While eating slowly and relaxing around food is simple in concept, it can be quite challenging to follow through with. I have noticed that this is one of the hardest changes for my clients to make. It has likely taken you a lifetime of fast eating to get to this point, so be gentle with yourself as you learn to become a slow eater. You have three meals a day plus snacks to practice slowing down, and each time you slow down, you take one more step toward improving your health. You may be surprised to find that what you thought of as food sensitivity or poor digestion may have actually been your body's sensitivity to eating too fast, not chewing well, or being overly stressed. I am now able to eat slowly about ninety percent of the time (it does not have to be perfect), and when I do, my digestion always runs much more smoothly and I feel nourished by my food rather than overstuffed. Slow down your pace today and your body will thank you. If it is challenging, be kind to yourself through the process and keep practicing. You will get the hang of it eventually.

Relaxed Eating Overview

Key Practice Steps:

1. Learn to become a relaxed eater. Have patience; it may take a little while.

2. Enjoy your food, chewing thoroughly and pausing between bites.

3. Eat a nourishing breakfast and lunch. Avoid skipping meals.

Your Personal Goal: _____

_____

_____

_____

_____

_____

_____

"Eating in the state of parasympathetic nervous system dominance—the relaxation response—is the hidden key to our most powerful nutritional metabolism. Biology insists on relaxed, pleasured, nourished eating."

- Marc David, bestselling author and founder of the Institute for the Psychology of Eating

3

Hydration

Affirmation:
*"I drink plenty of water to nourish
and cleanse my body."*

A simple, cost effective, and necessary way to make sure you are taking care of yourself is to drink plenty of filtered water. Our bodies are comprised of a very high percentage of water that needs to be continuously replenished. While we can survive weeks without food, our bodies can last only days without water. Water is imperative on so many levels. It lubricates the joints, regulates digestion and metabolism, helps the organs to function, keeps the body feeling energetic, reduces stress, reduces headaches, and much more. If you are someone who is chronically dehydrated, you will feel dramatically healthier when you commit to hydrating properly every day.

As a sensitive soul, you may be more prone to dehydration than the general population because you are more likely to be overstimulated during your daily activities. This overstimulation means that your nervous system ends up working overtime, potentially causing increased sweating, a faster heart rate and faster breathing, all of which can lead to dehydration. You are also more likely to be sensitive to temperature, both hot and cold, and specifically hot weather can leave you feeling dizzy, unbalanced, and then dehydrated.

Drinking water is vital regardless of your typical level of thirst. You might be surprised to learn that many people actually mistake the feeling of thirst for hunger. Years ago, I would feel what I thought was extreme hunger in the middle of the night, but if I drank a glass of water, the sensation was magically quenched. I realized I was actually mistaking my thirst for hunger. Next time you feel hungry at an unusual time, have a glass of water and see what happens.

While counterintuitive, if you are someone who rarely feels thirsty, this actually could be a sign that you are dehydrated and need to increase your water intake. Those who are chronically dehydrated can actually lose the sensation of thirst. Drink a tall glass of water when you wake up in the morning, and keep a water bottle with you throughout your day. If you drink enough, you will eventually regain the sensation of thirst. If you are sensitive to the taste of water, you can make your water more flavorful by adding a lemon, lime, orange, cucumber, mint, or even berries. This is also a nice way to add a little more sustenance to the water

When it comes to the "correct" quantity of water, everyone's needs are slightly different, but a general rule is approximately sixty-four ounces a day, adding more for days when you are sweating, drinking caffeine or alcohol, or feeling particularly stressed. The larger you are, the more water you will need. Because of your tendency to become overstimulated and dehydrated, you may likely need even more than the typical sixty-four ounces. I recommend keeping notes or using an app to help you track how much water you have had throughout the day. If I have a day where I am at home, I will fill up a large pitcher in the morning and make sure I finish it by the end of the day. Another easy way to tell if you are dehydrated is to check the color of your urine. It should be clear or pale yellow, not bright yellow, unless you are taking a supplement that can affect your urine color, such as a high dose of vitamin C or B-12.

Water quality is also significant. Tap water can contain many chemicals that you do not want to be exposed to daily, especially chlorine and fluoride, and as a sensitive soul, you are more likely to be affected by, or at least notice, the effects of these compounds. Bottled water is also not ideal for many reasons. The standards for bottled water are generally lower than tap water, so purity is not a guarantee. Bottled water is expensive, it is bad for the environment, and the plastic in the bottle can actually leach into your water, especially if it becomes heated (avoid leaving plastic water bottles in a hot car or out in the sun). Drinking filtered water is best.

I highly recommend using a filter that you install directly onto your faucet, as these types of filters are the most convenient and generally the most comprehensive when it comes to removing toxins from the water. Pitcher filters like Brita are more effective for taste improvement rather than true filtration. Regardless of the filter, make sure to change the filter on schedule, as an old filter can end up increasing the toxicity level rather than reducing it. To help increase your water intake, get your own water bottle to carry with you throughout the day. A glass bottle is the healthiest option and the easiest to clean. If water intake is a challenge for you, consider prioritizing this more highly as it is simple, easy and free and can make a dramatic shift in your wellbeing.

Hydration Overview

Key Practice Steps:

1. Drink approximately sixty-four ounces or more of water each day.

2. Filter your water.

3. Keep water with you throughout your day.

Your Personal Goal: _____

_____

_____

_____

_____

_____

_____

"Drinking water is like taking a shower
on the inside of your body."

-Author Unknown

4

Posture

Affirmation:
*"I hold my body in positions
of comfort and strength."*

How we hold our bodies in the world makes an incredible impact on both our physical and emotional wellbeing. As a sensitive soul, you may be shy about showing yourself and your heart to the world. You may be more likely to feel that the world is unsafe and that you need to protect yourself from others. This can lead to unhealthy postural habits that develop unconsciously. These habits progress over many years and become so deeply ingrained that they can be very hard to break.

For me, this desire to shield myself unintentionally led to slightly rounding my back and shoulders. It also led to a lack of eye contact and a steady gaze at the ground in an unconscious attempt to protect myself and not be seen. It was not until I found yoga that I even considered my posture and the ways it could affect my wellbeing. I was excited to learn that it is possible to teach yourself to feel mentally stronger just by how you hold your body.

In addition to the mental effects of poor posture, there are clear and damaging physical effects. Most chronic pain develops because of poor posture, especially poor posture that is repeated frequently. Even if you are not feeling any symptoms from misalignment now, over time, it can become a heavy burden on your body and overall wellbeing. Due to my past postural habits, I struggle on and off with neck and back pain and have to be very aware of my posture at all times or I will likely get a flare-up.

It is important to keep in mind that attention to posture is not simply something to think about during a yoga class or while getting your picture taken. It is a 24/7 practice. Your goal is to be in a healthy position as often as possible. I recommend first thinking about the most typical positions you spend long periods of time in. This may be sitting at a desk, driving a car, sleeping, or another kind of repetitive motion due to your job. Simply bringing more awareness to your posture is an important step. Without the awareness, no change can be made.

For proper alignment, you first need to learn how to stand in correct posture. In yoga, we call this Mountain Pose. Stand up in front of a mirror in your typical posture and notice what you look like. Now, pay attention to your body, starting at the feet. Your feet should be about hip distance apart and parallel. Watch that the toes are not turning in or out. The arches should be lifted and not collapsed. (The arches are actually muscles and it is beneficial to practice lifting your toes up and holding to build strength). Your legs should be straight. If you tend to lock your knees, practice unlocking them. The bend that you make to unlock them should be so slight that it is not actually a visible bend.

Next, pay attention to your pelvis. The pelvis should be neutral, not tipped forward with an over-arched low back, or tipped back with a flattened low back. There should be a natural curve in the lower spine. To find this neutral position, imagine bringing the pubic bone toward the tailbone and the tailbone simultaneously toward the public bone while engaging your lower abdominals slightly.

The shoulders should lift up, back, and then down, leaving the chest open, but not in a ridged way. Let your arms dangle. Your head should hover right on top of your cervical spine, which will have an inward curve. Make sure you are gazing forward and not up or down, as that would increase the tension on your neck. Imagine the crown of your head floating up toward the ceiling. Notice how you feel. This may sound like a lot of steps just to stand correctly, but once you get accustomed to it, it will feel natural and intuitive rather than overly complicated.

As an experiment, stand up and slouch your shoulders, then round your spine and look down. Notice how you feel both physically and mentally. Now try this again with confidence. Stand up, neutralize the pelvis, slightly engage your abdomen, lift your shoulders up to your ears and allow them to drop down, and let your head rest over your spine. Gaze forward and take a deep breath from this confident place. Next time you are not feeling confident or strong, change your posture, and notice how your mind and body shift in accordance.

Due to the fact that so many of us sit for most of the day, it is crucially important to apply these techniques to sitting as well. When sitting at a desk, make sure your feet are weight bearing on the floor with your thighs parallel to the ground. Set up your computer so that you can comfortably gaze straight forward at your screen. If your feet don't touch the ground, place something solid underneath your feet so that they are bearing weight. Place a pillow behind your lower back to support your lumbar curve. Make sure to get up and move around at least every forty-five minutes. Also, be very aware of your posture when using your cell phone so that you don't develop "text neck." Looking down at your phone constantly puts an enormous amount of unnecessary stress on your spine.

Pay attention to how you carry weight throughout your day. For years, I carried a heavy bag only on my right shoulder. I heard many times that you should switch which side you carry your bag on, but the importance of that did not sink in enough for me to change my habit. It felt more comfortable to stick with the same side I was used to. Little did I know, I was creating an imbalance in my back and looked in the mirror one day to find that my right shoulder was significantly lower than my left, contributing to my chronic back pain. With careful attention, physical therapy and a good chiropractor, I have mostly resolved the imbalance, but it would have been much easier to avoid this situation in the first place. If this is the case for you, make sure to even out how you carry your bag, or better yet, use a backpack or something that allows you to support the weight equally between sides. If you have young children, make sure to switch which side you hold them on. Always bend your knees if you reach down to pick something (or someone) up.

Due to the great length of time we spend in our bed each night, it is also crucial to be aware of how you sleep. Make sure you have a comfortable mattress and pillow. You want your neck to be neutral when you sleep, so make sure your pillow is high enough that your head is not tilted down but low enough that it is not tilted up. Attempt to sleep on your back, your side, or a combination of the two. When you sleep on your side it is helpful to place a pillow in between your knees to keep your spine in alignment. Sleeping on your stomach can greatly increase tension in the body, especially the neck, so it's helpful to try to avoid it.

The best way to make sure you are living with good posture is to do a posture check periodically throughout the day, every day. Your sensitive body will thank you and your sensitive soul will feel more empowered, healthy, and strong.

Weakened Posture vs. Empowered Posture

Posture Overview

Key Practice Steps:

1. Notice your posture periodically throughout the day.

2. Hold your body in positions of alignment and strength.

3. Get up and move around at least every forty-five minutes, except when sleeping.

Your Personal Goal: _____

_____

_____

_____

_____

_____

_____

"A good stance and posture reflect
a proper state of mind."

-Morihei Ueshiba

5

Joyful Movement

Affirmation:
"I move my body with pleasure and joy."

Our bodies need to be nurtured and taken care of and they also need to move. A sedentary lifestyle is certainly one of the biggest risk factors for an unhealthy mind and body, but that does not mean that you need to run marathons to be healthy. As a sensitive soul, you may find that extremely strenuous exercise actually overexerts you. Instead, it is important to focus on movement that makes you feel joy, pleasure, and freedom in your body.

In my coaching practice, I have noticed that many people force themselves to undergo strenuous exercise that they actually hate in the name of weight loss or good health. For the majority of sensitive people, strenuous exercise, if done out of force or punishment, can actually have a detrimental effect. If you hate every minute of your workout, what kind of message is that going to send to your body? Your body is likely going to go into a physiological stress response, which will likely slow down your metabolism and leave you feeling anxious. You could have gone for a happy walk in the woods and been better off.

You also have a much greater chance of sticking to an exercise routine that you find enjoyable. The goal is for your movement practice to help you feel more embodied, not to make you hate being in your body, as overly vigorous exercise often does. If you love strenuous exercise then by all means, continue on, but make sure you are doing it for the right reasons.

If you could pick any kind of movement to practice, what would you choose? The answer to this question is the key to the best exercise and movement practice for you. For me, I love practicing yoga and dancing. Neither feels stressful to me. They are activities I do for pure joy. When in doubt, walking is a wonderful form of exercise. Do you love dance? Then dance. Capoeira? Then try that. Biking? You get the idea. The best exercise for you is a practice that you like so much that you can do it with a sense of joy and freedom in your body. Remember, you do not need to move for two hours a day for it to be worthwhile. If you haven't been in the routine of moving frequently, start by committing to even ten minutes a day. A little bit of movement is far better than none.

For sensitive souls like us, working on core strength is beneficial too. Our core is what gives us our sense of confidence—it protects our organs and holds us together. Work on your core and you will find that you sit and stand more easily, and you will feel more confident in who you are. Prioritizing core work has been helpful in my own process of becoming strong and empowered.

It is also helpful to take an honest look at your strengths and weaknesses. We tend to gravitate toward what we are already skilled at. For example, I know many yogis who are extremely flexible but need to work a little more on their strength, and many weight lifters who are remarkably strong but lack flexibility. Adding even a small amount of something you need to work on can make a big difference and help you to feel more balanced and whole. Whatever you choose, remember to always move your body out of love rather than for punishment or torture.

Joyful Movement Overview

Key Practice Steps:

1. Move your body often, even if for just ten minutes.
2. Find movement practices you enjoy and move your body for pleasure rather than punishment.
3. Work on any physical weaknesses.

Your Personal Goal: _____

_____

_____

_____

_____

_____

_____

"Movement is the song of the body."

-Vanda Scaravelli

6
Slowing Down

Affirmation:
"I move through my day at a calm and relaxed pace. I have all the time I need."

Rushing and being overscheduled has become so common in our culture that many of us do not even know we are suffering from this frantic way of life. I noticed one day that I was rushing through practically everything I did. I was hurried while eating, walking, cleaning, and driving. Even my yoga practice felt a bit rushed. I constantly felt like I didn't have enough time. I could feel the stress this was causing me and knew I had to slow down.

As a sensitive soul, it is likely that you feel easily stressed or overwhelmed from being busy or rushing, too. Maybe you feel like you are never able to do all that you need to do. I know that when my fatigue was at its worst, I was actually more likely to rush because I felt I had such limited time in my day. This rushing, though, caused me to become more fatigued, so it created a vicious cycle.

Do you feel like you are in a constant state of rush? If so, do you enjoy rushing? I have noticed time and time again that those who rush are anxious, unsettled, and not particularly happy. They have trouble sitting still, are usually overwhelmed, and feel as though there is never enough time in the day. Rushing literally signals the nervous system that something is wrong and that you are in danger even when you are actually safe. This creates a state of stress, which may lead to any number of symptoms including headaches, sweating, dry mouth, digestive upset, difficulty breathing, palpitations, disturbed sleep, difficulty concentrating, mood issues, and more. When experienced chronically, stress can lead to disease.

One reason why we rush is because of a perceived lack of time. When we constantly tell ourselves that we "don't have enough time," we are actually increasing our sense of stress and urgency, which makes time seem to move faster. Instead, try saying to yourself, "I have all the time I need," and notice how that helps you to relax. Gay Hendricks in his book, *The Big Leap*, talks about avoiding complaining about time, which I find extremely helpful. I used to always find myself thinking, "I wish I had more time," which created a feeling of stress and deficiency. Instead say, "I am grateful for the time I have. I always have enough time," which creates appreciation, and in turn, a sense of ease. He also recommends avoiding using time as an excuse. We often say, "I don't have time to do that," when we really mean, "This is not my priority in this moment," or, "I do not want to do that." Be honest with your reasoning and notice how not blaming time feels more genuine and relaxed.

If you are a busy person, you may be resistant to slowing down, but it is most likely exactly what you need to do. There is incredible healing power in slowing down. We so often resist what we need most because it is uncomfortable, especially at first. In most cases, it is a matter of practice, patience, and getting past those first few tries. Notice what tasks you do in a rushed way and commit to slowing them down. Bring your attention to your breath as frequently as possible. Try walking slower, talking slower, and leaving more time to get where you are going. Too many of us are sprinting through the marathon of life. What would happen if you were to attempt to sprint a marathon? You would inevitably burn out before the first mile. Avoid this burn out in your life and slow down the pace.

Committing to slowing down and taking your time more regularly will not only make you feel much healthier, but you will appreciate life more and find joy in many little things that you did not even take time to notice before. Take moments each day to pause, breathe, and simply exist without rushing off to the next thing. Make a list of the activities that you generally rush through so that you can bring extra awareness to them as you go about your day. Be gentle with your sensitive self as you practice and take it one day at a time. I find that I still have to remind myself at least once or twice a day to slow down. It is a lifelong practice, but anytime you remember to slow down you are bringing consciousness to the situation and taking your health back into your own hands. Be grateful for remembering rather than beating yourself up for forgetting.

Slowing Down Overview

Key Practice Steps:

1. Commit to slowing down your daily life.

2. Notice where you tend to rush and pay extra attention during those moments. Avoid blaming time.

3. Periodically pause and bring your attention to your breath if you notice yourself rushing.

Which activities in your life do you tend to rush through?

- _____
- _____
- _____

Your Personal Goal: _____

_____

_____

_____

_____

"Nature does not hurry, and yet
everything is accomplished."

-Lao Tzu

7
Breathing

Affirmation:
"As I inhale, I take in fresh new energy. As I exhale, I let go of what is no longer serving me."

Breathing is a fundamental element of life that we often overlook and take for granted. Our breath is our life force energy and our connection between mind and body. We can live for weeks without food, days without water, but only minutes without air. Oxygen is the most important nutrient of all. Take a moment to notice your breath and feel the oxygen coming into your lungs. Exhale and release what is no longer serving you.

Like many sensitive souls, you may be accustomed to breathing shallow breaths, often due to a feeling of overstimulation in the nervous system. The good news is you have the power to use your breath as a tool to calm your nervous system and empower yourself in the present moment. As you change your relationship to your breath, you change how you experience your life. Begin right now by making your breathing more life affirming and complete.

As you start paying more attention to your breath, you will discover that simply by paying attention, your breathing will naturally begin to shift without effort. The more you can bring awareness to it, the more you can step back into using more of your lung capacity. Make sure your natural breath is through your nose rather than your mouth. The nose has a superior filtration system and it is also better at supplying the necessary oxygen to the brain and body. However, an occasional long exhale through the mouth is a great way to relieve tension and stress.

The breath is directly connected to the nervous system. Long exhales promote relaxation and inhales promote stimulation. I have found a direct correlation between the state of the breath and the state of anxiety for my clients. The ones who are the most anxious are constantly holding their breath and breathing shallow breaths. The ones who are the most relaxed take slow, calm breaths. It is amazing to see this connection. Notice this in yourself and those you come in contact with.

Relaxed breathing can also be helpful when trying to fall asleep. You can either practice long exhales through both nostrils, or long exhales only through the left nostril. The left nostril is linked to your parasympathetic nervous system and will help you relax, while the right nostril is linked to your sympathetic nervous system and offers a more stimulating effect.

There are many different yogic breathing practices you can experiment with including practicing long exhalations, three-part breathing, alternate nostril breathing, and Lion's Breath. The first step of any of these breathing exercises is to find a comfortable position to sit or lie down.

Long Exhalations

You can create a calming effect by breathing out for a longer period of time than you breathe in for. Try counting to four on your inhalation and six on your exhalation. Allow this long exhale to help you let go and relax. You are welcome to make the count longer or shorter depending on your own personal breath cycle, but try to keep a similar ratio, with the exhale longer than the inhale. For example, inhaling for the count of six and exhaling for eight, or inhaling for three and exhaling for five would both be appropriate alternatives.

Three-Part Breath

This breath helps you to use more of your long capacity than you typically use. Begin by inhaling deeply, allowing the belly to rise. Then, expand the rib cage. Finally, lift the chest. Practice this one step at a time. On your exhalation, let the breath out slowly, starting with your chest, then your rib cage, and finally back to your belly. You can imagine that you are blowing up a balloon in your torso on your inhalation, and that the air is being let out of the balloon on the exhalation. Continue to repeat this breath for about five minutes or until you feel complete.

Alternate Nostril Breathing

This is a great harmonizing breath as it balances the two hemispheres of the brain. Begin by taking your right hand to your nose and closing your right nostril with your thumb. Now inhale through your left nostril. At the end of the inhalation, close the left nostril with your ring finger, release your thumb, and exhale through your right nostril. Next, inhale through your right nostril, then close your right nostril with your thumb, release your ring finger, and exhale through your left nostril. This is one round. You will continue to inhale left, exhale right, inhale right and exhale left for at least 4 more rounds or until you feel complete.

Lion's Breath

Lion's Breath is quick and helpful to let out unnecessary tension when you don't have a lot of time. Simply inhale deeply through your nose, and then exhale strongly through your mouth while sticking your tongue out and making a forceful "aahhhh" sound. The sound should resemble the sound of thirst being quenched. Repeat this breath approximately four times in a row and then rest.

Take time to experiment and see which exercises you like most. Remember, conscious breathing does not need to always be done as a formal practice or on a meditation cushion. You can bring attention to your breath practically any time, such as while waiting in line, driving, or listening to someone speak. There are countless opportunities to breathe more fully each and every day.

Breathing Overview

Key Practice Steps:

1. Periodically bring attention to your breath throughout your day, especially when feeling stressed.

2. Learn different breathing exercises and techniques to improve the quality of your breath.

3. Practice your breathing to help you sleep.

Your Personal Goal: _____

_____

_____

_____

_____

_____

_____

"Breath is essential to life. If you only
half breathe, you only half live."

-Author Unknown

8

Relaxation

Affirmation:
"My body is calm and relaxed."

It is now well known that stress plays a major factor in practically all diseases and health conditions. Even with this knowledge, relaxation is still not valued highly in our achievement-based culture. However, that does not mean that you cannot choose to value it highly for yourself. In fact, to live a long and happy life, relaxation must be made a priority because it is during a relaxation response that all healing takes place. When you relax, you reduce stress in the body, your heart rate slows down, and your blood pressure reduces. When you are relaxed, you sleep better, breathe better, and digest your food better. You can think better, make more sound decisions, and your memory improves. The more you relax, the more opportunity you give your body to heal itself naturally.

As a sensitive soul, you may likely find that you need more relaxation in your life than those around you. You may be more affected by stimulation and require more peace and quiet. This is not something to feel bad about, rather it is something to embrace. I spent a lot of time fighting my need for rest and relaxation and feeling guilty about it. It made me feel like something was wrong with me. When I learned to accept the fact that I need more rest and downtime than what is considered "normal," I was able to enjoy the rest more, get more out of it, and feel better about who I am as a person. I also believe that most people actually need more rest, but that they tend to ignore their body's signals and use stimulants to override their fatigue. As a sensitive soul, you are more in touch with those signals and overriding your feelings is not beneficial to you. Know that it is normal and healthy to need rest and relaxation.

There are many wonderful forms of relaxation. Everyone is unique so it is helpful to experiment with the type of relaxation that works for you. I teach and practice restorative yoga—a gentle, opening practice of holding the body in extremely comfortable postures, propped with blankets and bolsters. The comfort of the postures allows relaxation to envelop you without force or strain. This is a great practice for anyone, especially those who suffer from fatigue, chronic stress, or who are dealing with injuries. One of my favorite restorative yoga postures that does not require yoga props is called "legs up the couch." You simply place a yoga mat or comfortable blanket in front of a couch or soft chair and lie down on the floor with your legs bent over the couch. This mild inversion helps calm the nervous system and gives your body and mind a much needed break. Practice this pose for approximately ten to fifteen minutes or until you become uncomfortable. If you are uncomfortable, the restorative postures will lose their benefit because you won't be able to fully relax. Therefore, it is imperative to make sure you are as comfortable as possible.

Yin yoga, which is a practice of long held passive stretching of the connective tissue, is also an excellent form of relaxation. It is more challenging than restorative yoga, so if you are new to yoga, I recommend starting first with restorative. Besides good old sleep, restorative yoga and yin yoga are my go-to ways to relax. The breathing exercises we learned in the previous section (except for Lion's Breath) are also excellent ways to relax.

Meditation is a wonderful practice to not only relax the body but to also to connect with your inner wisdom and ease your mind. There are many techniques to use and so it is likely that you will be able to find one that is right for you. I recommend taking a group class to get professional instruction. Meditating in a group is helpful because the energy of the teacher and the group holds the space and creates an enhanced environment to quiet the mind. There are also many different apps and websites that have meditation tracks to help guide you while you are getting started.

One option to help you start meditating is the "So Hum" mantra. As you sit in mediation, on your inhale, think the word "So," and on your exhale, think the word "Hum." Then repeat this mantra for at least five minutes. I also enjoy the mantra, "I'm breathing in," on the inhalation, and, "I'm breathing out," on the exhalation. I find meditation to be incredibly soothing, especially when I am feeling alert. If I am feeling tired, I usually save mediation for when I am rested so that I can focus more effectively. When first starting out, meditation can actually feel more aggravating than helpful, so make sure you go into it with an open mind, knowing that it takes time to become skilled at it. The more you practice, the more you will experience the benefits.

Guided relaxation is also a wonderful way to relax with more structure and direction. Depending on the guide, you may be led through a full body scan or on a mental journey through a beautiful place. The body responds extremely well to thoughts about a relaxing experience. Even just imagining a peaceful experience clearly can help you to feel the same benefit as if you were actually there. This can be a great practice for when you are alert, but you can also practice when you are tired as it can actually help you fall asleep. In addition to helping you relax, guided relaxation and imagery can also be used to help achieve goals such as quitting a bad habit and reducing pain. There are many apps and websites that have guided relaxation tracks so you can likely find one that is tailored to your personal goal.

Keep in mind as you are choosing a relaxation practice that activities like watching a movie, playing with your phone, or even reading may be enjoyable but they do not count as your relaxation for the day. The most important part of your relaxation is that you are allowing your body and mind to rest, and those activities are too mentally stimulating to get the desired benefit of a calm and peaceful mind.

If you are not able to do a more formal relaxation practice, even taking five minutes to lie down on your bed and feel your body is an effective relaxation technique. Once you get accustomed to practicing relaxation, you will find that it is no longer on your "to-do" list, but actually something you get excited about. Start with five minutes a day and then gradually increase to at least twenty minutes a day. If you feel you do not have time or that relaxation is too challenging for you, then that is all the more reason it is essential to practice.

Learning to relax may take more practice than you realize, but it is worth it. The more you can relax and nurture your sensitive body, the more whole and complete you will feel and the more you will be able to move through life with confidence and ease.

Relaxation Overview

Key Practice Steps:

1. Prioritize daily relaxation.

2. Experiment with different types of relaxation until you find one that suits you.

3. When you feel there is "no time," remind yourself of the importance of relaxation and practice anyway.

Your Personal Goal: _____

_____

_____

_____

_____

_____

_____

"You should sit in meditation for twenty
minutes a day, unless you're too busy,
then you should sit for an hour."

-Zen proverb

9

Nature

Affirmation:
"I am one with nature."

As a sensitive soul, it is likely that you feel a strong connection to nature and natural beauty. The land is our home and the more we can be with Mother Earth, the more we remember that we are part of nature too. Breathing fresh air and enjoying the warmth of the sun can much more easily melt away a negative feeling and give you a fresh outlook than stale indoor air can.

Depending on the season and where you live, days and even weeks can go by without spending quality time outside. You may be working inside all day and not have the opportunity to get outside or take advantage of the daylight. As often as you can, prioritize going outside by scheduling walks, runs, picnics, hikes, time to sit on a bench, trips to the beach, bike rides, star gazing, or anything that gets you enjoying the fresh air. Consider if there is anything you can do outside that you might normally do inside, such as eating lunch or making a phone call.

I have a sensitive client from Boston who struggled with seasonal affective disorder. She felt generally okay during the spring, summer and early fall, but when it came to winter, she became depressed and would not leave her house for days at a time—what she called "hibernating." After a particularly bad winter and with my encouragement, she decided she'd had enough, packed up her things, and moved to a warmer climate. She is now able to enjoy nature and fresh air daily and she says that she finally feels like her true self again. It was a difficult decision, but it ended up being exactly what she needed to regain her strength and confidence. The ability to enjoy being outside truly makes a world of difference. Is this something that needs to change for you?

To increase your connection to nature at home, I recommend opening your blinds in the morning when you wake up, opening the windows to spread fresh air throughout the house, and keeping houseplants to help filter the air. Investing in an air filter is also beneficial. When you feel overwhelmed or anxious and cannot shake it, go outside and let the fresh air help you gain a new perspective.

Another key aspect of healing through nature is the practice of grounding or "earthing," meaning placing your bare skin (usually the bottoms of the feet) on the earth. Earth's energy is hugely beneficial for our health. When we touch the earth, we receive a charge of energy that immediately improves our wellbeing. Our modern lifestyle keeps us inside most of the time, and when we do go outside, we are almost always wearing shoes, which block the absorption of this beneficial energy. Many people do not ever directly connect to the earth. Going barefoot outside is the easiest and most effective way to improve your wellbeing, and it is totally free. There are also grounding products, such as footpads, sheets, and shoes that you can use when you are unable to ground outside. Consistent grounding has the ability to decrease symptoms of chronic conditions, decrease inflammation, slow the process of aging, and help people to lead more energetic and healthy lives.

Even if you cannot go outside, can you look out the window and notice the clouds in the sky? Can you take time to be aware of when the sun sets and the current phase of the moon? Do you have a tall tree outside of your office or house that you can periodically gaze at? Even simply looking at images of the beauty of nature can be healing. The beach is my happy place, so I love looking at beautiful beach photos as well as photos of majestic mountains and colorful sunsets. There are so many beautiful images online to take advantage of when not in nature. These are good backups when you can't go outside, but make sure you prioritize the real thing. Allow the healing forces of nature to revitalize you as often as possible.

Nature Overview

Key Practice Steps:

1. Spend time outside daily.

2. Take a minute each day to see and appreciate the trees, the sun, the sky, the stars and the moon.

3. Breathe plenty of fresh air every day and ground into the earth whenever possible.

Your Personal Goal: _____

_____

_____

_____

_____

_____

_____

"Nature is painting for us, day after day,
pictures of infinite beauty if only we have
the eyes to see them."

-John Ruskin

10
Sleep

Affirmation:
"My sleep is restful, rhythmic, and deep."

Everyone knows how bad it feels to be sleep deprived, so why is it that our culture looks upon getting a lot of sleep as being lazy or a waste of time? Somehow, being sleep deprived has become a virtue. As a sensitive soul, you may find that you need more sleep than most or that you need daily naps to rejuvenate, and that is okay. In fact, it is extremely healthy for you. During sleep, your brain is essentially being cleaned, removing what is not serving you or causing blockages, and allowing you to wake up with a fresh mindset. You can think of sleep as the time when your body takes out your mental trash. When we do not get enough sleep, we wake up feeling rusty because some of the trash has not been removed. Over time, lack of sleep creates a buildup of this mental trash in your brain, causing you to not feel fully refreshed or alert. You may lose the ability to think clearly and have trouble going about your daily activities without a stimulant. Eventually, this can lead to total exhaustion, excessive stress, and can even contribute to disease. No matter how many times you hear someone say, "I'll sleep when I'm dead," depriving yourself of sleep is not a healthy way to live. It is essential to prioritize your sleep for a full and meaningful experience on Earth.

For sleep consistency and quality, it is highly beneficial to wake up at the same time every day so that your body can get into a proper circadian rhythm. You also want to try to go to bed at the same time as often as possible for the same reason. Sleeping somewhere between seven and nine hours a night is usually perfect for most people. In the long term, sleeping less than seven hours a night will not provide the proper brain cleaning needed for a healthy body and mind.

Our sleep progresses in approximately ninety-minute cycles. If you wake up in the middle of a cycle when your sleep is the deepest, you may find yourself feeling groggier and less rested than you would at the end of your cycle. Therefore, it is recommended to sleep in multiple ninety-minute cycles. For example, it would likely be best to sleep for seven and a half hours (five full cycles of ninety-minutes) rather than eight hours, which would leave you waking up in the middle of your sixth cycle. This can be a bit hard to track, especially if you suffer from bouts of insomnia or if your sleep cycles happen to be a bit more or less than ninety minutes, but for many people, it works extremely well. I recommend giving it a try to see if you notice any benefit. There are also different sleep apps you can use to track your sleep cycles.

I had a client who struggled daily with getting up in the morning in time for work. We set her on a schedule of waking up at the same time every day with either five or six sleep cycles, depending on her obligations the previous evening. It took a little while, but once she stuck to the schedule, she said she felt much more rested in the morning and actually even looked forward to getting out of bed. It definitely takes dedication to stick to a sleep schedule, but it is certainly worth it in the end if you feel more rested and alert throughout your day. Why not at least try it for a week or two and see what happens? You can always go back to your old routine.

As a sensitive soul, you will want to create a supportive, calm sleep environment. It is best to sleep in a dark, cool room with optional white noise from a sound machine or fan if you are a light sleeper. Limit any electronics in the room, especially a cell phone near your head. Your cell phone can actually interfere with the process of cleaning out the brain. Blue lights emanating from electronics can promote wakefulness, so it is best to remove them from the room altogether. If you are sensitive to light, I also recommend sleeping with an eye mask. As a sensitive soul, I like to remove all electronics from my room, tidy my space before I fall asleep, put on my eye mask, and use a body pillow between my knees to provide a comfortable and calming sleep experience.

If you have trouble falling asleep, it is usually because you have difficulty getting your mind to relax. In that case, developing a bedtime ritual is very valuable. There are many different techniques you can try, so start by thinking of something you enjoy doing that helps you relax. I enjoy journaling and reading before bed. Journaling gives me the opportunity to get out how I feel and to write down what I need to remember for the following day so that I can then rest my head in peace. Reading an inspiring book helps me bring positivity into my mind before I fall asleep and helps to tire my eyes. You can also try restorative yoga, conscious breathing, taking a bath, or listening to a relaxation track.

Another effective tool to help you fall asleep is to practice a body scan. In a slow, methodical way, you bring attention to each area of your body, one at a time. Start with your toes and then slowly move your relaxed attention upward, imagining each area getting totally relaxed as you bring your awareness to it. Once you reach the crown of your head, then you can feel your whole body relaxed all at once. I have used this technique countless times to help me sleep and I find that I rarely even reach my head because I have already fallen asleep.

In addition to a bedtime ritual, I find that it is extremely helpful to also have a morning ritual. How you start your day will be a reflection of the quality of the rest of your day, so it is important to start your day off right. I used to be one to press the snooze button multiple times before getting up because no matter what time it was, I never felt refreshed and ready to start the day. I realized, though, that when I allowed myself to lay in bed longer, I always felt much worse than when I motivated myself to get right out of bed. It was no easier to get up fifteen minutes later, and then I had to rush getting ready, which led me to feel more tired all day.

I highly recommend sticking to your wake up time and getting up with a plan. I love to go for a walk, do yoga, or shower right when I get up. Whatever you choose to do, make sure you do not check your email first. This will be a slippery slope, leading your whole day to be framed by reaction rather than action. Instead, do something healthy and revitalizing when you wake up. Make a plan for your morning the night before and stick with that plan.

While prioritizing sleep is a simple idea that everyone knows they need to do, it can be hard to put into practice. Is this something you need to work on? Take a moment to write down how refreshed you would feel if you got more sleep, then schedule it in. You may feel too old to have a bedtime, but part of being an adult is learning to be an excellent parent to yourself. Prioritize your wellbeing over the desire to be up late or sleep in and set a time and stick to it. If you end up not getting enough sleep, then try your best to make time for a nap or some deep relaxation during your day. Embrace the rest your body needs.

Sleep Overview

Key Practice Steps:

1. Prioritize your sleep. Create a morning and an evening ritual.
2. Wake up at the same time every day and avoid snoozing.
3. Sleep in a cool, dark, comfortable room.

Your Personal Goal: _____

_____

_____

_____

_____

_____

_____

"Sleep is the golden chain that ties
health and our bodies together."

-Thomas Dekker

11
Cut Back on Chemicals

Affirmation:
*"I consciously choose healthy and
natural products for my body and home."*

I was born with a strong sense of smell and heightened awareness for toxic chemicals, which has only increased with age. For example, I cannot walk into the perfume section of a department store without immediately feeling like my face is going to break out in hives. While another shopper may say, "This smells amazing!" all I smell are chemicals. Everyday activities like washing the dishes can make me uncomfortable and itchy if I use products many would consider "normal" like Dawn or Ajax. I am even sensitive to most toilet paper because the majority of what is readily available has been treated with bleach or a similar chemical.

As a sensitive soul, you are likely more affected by chemicals, pesticides, perfumes, dyes, and other unnatural substances too. Have you ever put on perfume only to find it gave you a headache or made you itchy? Have you ever walked into a room that had just been cleaned with chemicals and felt like you couldn't breathe? While I know it can be frustrating to be so sensitive, I also like to think of it as a bonus early warning sign. These substances are not healthy for anyone, even those who do not appear to be sensitive to them, so it is better that you are finding out sooner than later and are able to begin removing these items from your life. I know that because of my sensitivity to chemicals, I have been able to actively avoid them and I am much healthier today than I otherwise would have been. I'd take the early warning sign over the late one any day.

There are many ways to begin limiting your exposure to chemicals. First, as we discussed earlier, there is what you put **in** your body. You want to eat the most natural ingredients as regularly as possible and drink filtered water. Anything processed in a factory is likely to contain something unnatural for your body. You also want to think about what you put **on** your body. Did you know that chemicals that come in contact with the skin can actually be absorbed straight into your bloodstream? The skin is our biggest organ, is highly permeable, and does not have the same filtration system that the stomach does to get rid of toxic waste. This can lead to a lifetime of buildup of toxic chemicals in the body.

Start by looking at your body products such as lotions, shampoos, makeup, perfume, toothpaste, deodorant, etc. There are some really excellent organic products on the market—look for the labels "organic" and "fragrance-free." Choose products with fewer ingredients and ones you are familiar with. You can always look up ingredients if you are not sure. There are also all kinds of recipes online to make your own products. The ideal rule of thumb is to try not to put anything on your body that you could not eat, or as close to that as possible. For example, coconut oil makes for great skin moisturizer. If you are new to paying attention to chemicals in products, remember to pace yourself. Start with just being aware of the ingredients you are using and slowly try new, healthier alternatives.

Effective natural products can sometimes be hard to find,

but over time, I believe they will become easier and easier to find due to high demand from educated, health conscious people like yourself. I actually spent a few years trying to find a deodorant that both worked and had high quality ingredients. I recommend the brand Deodo Mom as it only has two ingredients (magnesium and water) and it works well for most people. I have found water with sea salt to be a fairly effective deodorant as well. Keep in mind that a deodorant will work better when you are wearing natural fabric like cotton as your perspiration will likely react more pungently with synthetic material.

Next, you can take a look at your household cleaning products. These (along with dryer sheets) are some of the most toxic items in your home. For help determining the quality of your products, visit the Environmental Working Group Website: EWG.org. If you get your house cleaned regularly, make sure to either find green cleaners or give your cleaning person healthy products to use. I also recommend avoiding antibacterial soap as this soap strips away all the good bacteria and most of the bad bacteria, leaving just the most harmful and resilient bacteria behind to multiply. There are also other major concerns about the safety of antibacterial soap including potential antibiotic resistance, danger to the environment, and a disruption in the endocrine system. Instead, consider using probiotic soap, which crowd out the bad bacteria and leave behind only healthy bacteria.

It is also important to take a look at the fabric your clothes are made of and begin moving away from synthetic materials and toward natural fiber materials such as cotton, linen, or silk. Fabrics such as polyester, acrylic, spandex, and rayon are made from joining chemicals together; essentially, they are the processed food of clothing. I never felt comfortable wearing certain clothes but did not know why. It wasn't until I started paying more attention to the fabrics I wore that I was able to notice the precise correlation between feeling uncomfortable and synthetic materials. Natural fabric is more sustainable, better for your health, and while it can be more expensive, it is actually a better investment because natural fiber materials generally last much longer (and they won't make you smell!).

This may feel like a huge undertaking, but the decision to at least limit chemicals should be an easy one. Do you care about the environment? Do you care about your health? If you answered yes to either or both of those questions, then you want to start switching to more natural products today. Remember that we are not separate from the environment. Any choice you make for the environment is a choice for your health and vice versa. If this is all new to you, I recommended starting small. When I decided to switch over to better quality products, I first threw out all of my old products out of excitement to start fresh, only to feel frustrated for the next few months while I slowly found and tested new products. Start with one or two at a time, buying a new natural product when you run out of your old toxic one. Some will work a lot better than others, so try not to be discouraged if one of them does not work out as you hoped. Keep in mind that the word "natural" does not have any set standards, so even if a product says "natural," you still want to do some research on the ingredients. Look for the organic seal, ingredients you know, and remember: the fewer ingredients, the better.

It is also important not to be too rigid with this. If there is a specific product that you are unwilling to give up, that is okay. Use your product and enjoy it guilt-free. Guilt and stress over this could end up being more harmful to your health than the chemicals themselves! My guilt-free beauty regimen of choice is getting my hair highlighted periodically. It makes me feel light, happy and free, and that feeling is worth it to me. Maybe you want to start with buying better quality food and are not ready to change your products yet. Take it one step at a time and allow whatever you choose to be okay.

Cut Back on Chemicals Overview

Key Practice Steps:

1. Use organic natural skin, hair, and beauty products as often as possible.

2. Use high quality natural cleaning products.

3. Pay attention to the fabric in your clothes.

Your Personal Goal: _____

_____

_____

_____

_____

_____

_____

"The first step in eliminating toxins and harmful chemicals in your home is to stop bringing in new ones."

-Samantha Hogan

12

Continue to Explore

Affirmation:
*"Every experience I have in my body is
an opportunity to learn and grow."*

The body is our temple and our home. As you grow and change, so will your body, and through various experiences and challenges throughout your life, you will have the opportunity to go deeper and learn more about your home. It is essential to continue to explore and to be curious about your body. One who knows and understands their body well will be the first to be able to recognize when something is wrong. As the sensitive being you are, you are generally more aware of subtleties in your body, and in turn, will have more opportunities to learn about your body throughout the course of your life.

I struggled for many years with extreme exhaustion and eye fatigue. I did not notice any change in my vision so I did not think to get my eyes tested. I assumed the eye pain was due to my chronic fatigue and found the only way to make my eyes feel better was to sleep. One day, I had a gut feeling to call the eye doctor and schedule an appointment. After only a brief exam, she found that I needed glasses! The prescription was minor enough that I had not specifically noticed, but I'd been unconsciously squinting throughout the day, which led to my daily eye pain. Once I started wearing glasses, my eye pain drastically reduced, and as you can imagine, this was a huge relief for me. I also struggled for years with low back and hip pain just from walking. Ever since getting orthotics from my local pedorthist, I have been completely free of that pain. Do you have something that has been bothering you that you have not fully looked into?

Often, a visit with a traditional Western doctor will not be enough to help you get to the bottom of what is ailing you. Try exploring many different healing modalities and see what resonates with you. A skilled chiropractor can help with many ailments, especially reducing back, neck and hip pain. Yoga has countless benefits including increased flexibility, greater muscle tone, improved breathing, and building a greater connection between the mind and body. Acupuncture can also be used for countless complaints and has been specifically acclaimed for reducing pain of all kinds. There are many other healing modalities that can also be highly effective including, but not limited to, physical therapy, reiki, bodywork, Ayurveda, reflexology, tai chi, and qi gong. Keep in mind that for the most part, healing takes time. You may be lucky and find a quick fix, but that quick fix is the exception rather than the rule. We frequently stumble upon a powerful healing modality, but do not stick to it long enough to allow it to work. Be patient and enjoy the process of understanding your sensitive body. There is always more to learn.

Continue to Explore Overview

Key Practice Steps:

1. Experiment with different healing modalities.

2. Stick to one modality long enough to see the results.

3. Take action when you feel something in the body is not functioning properly. The longer you wait, the bigger the problem is likely to become.

Your Personal Goal: _____

_____

_____

_____

_____

_____

_____

"Take care of your body.
It's the only place you have to live."

-Jim Rohn

PART 2

Heart

Affirmation:
"My heart is full of love."

While creating change through the body is an incredibly significant piece of healing and empowerment, the manner in which you do so is often even more significant. We cannot simply hate or force ourselves into change. If this is our mentality, eventually, we will go right back to how we were before and then beat ourselves up about it. All lasting change needs to be created and maintained through love. Let love guide you.

1
Self Love

Affirmation:
*"I love and accept myself.
I only speak kind words about myself."*

Learning to truly care for yourself requires that you learn to love and accept yourself exactly as you are. It is an autoimmune condition to be too hard on yourself—your body and mind are being attacked by your own negative thoughts! When you attack yourself, you become even less likely to love yourself. How can you love someone who attacks you? We regularly accept treatment from ourselves that we would absolutely not accept from someone else. This has to change. If it does not change, you will be stuck never feeling worthy or empowered no matter what you do. Forgive yourself for any past actions you have taken that you are not proud of and begin to cultivate an attitude of love and acceptance toward yourself today. There is no time to spare.

As a sensitive soul, you may likely struggle with truly loving yourself because you haven't yet learned of the genuine gifts of your sensitivity, and may be consciously or unconsciously viewing yourself as unusual or even weak. The older you get, the more you realize that being different is a good thing. How dull would life be if we were all exactly alike? How could we learn from each other? Instead of wanting to fit in to what you might perceive as "normal," you want to work toward being the most authentic, true version of yourself that you can be.

If the authentic you is sensitive, then embrace all of

your wonderful sensitive qualities. Think about it this way. If you took away your sensitivity, that would likely take away the essence of who you are. It would take away your strong intuition, your empathy, your passion, creativity, conscientiousness, and so much more. When I think of those things being taken away from me, I am reminded that I love those things about myself and couldn't imagine not having them. That's what makes me who I am. When you focus on what you have rather than what you don't have, your heart will fill with love and gratitude for who you are and it will be much easier to love yourself.

As a sensitive soul, you are more likely than others to deal with negative self-talk because of your tendency for perfectionism. You may want or feel that you need everything to go as you planned and to be perfect every time, which unfortunately, is not often realistic. This can cause you to feel unsatisfied with yourself for the tiny mistakes you make rather than focusing on feeling good about the other many things that you do quite well.

I developed this perfectionistic trait very early on in life. I remember being devastated in elementary school if I received a grade of A instead of the A+ I typically earned. It seemed that no matter how well I did, the bar would magically get higher right after any accomplishment. I never felt worthy because, to me, the only way to feel worthy was to be better than perfect, which of course, is impossible. This way of living was greatly unfulfilling. I have recognized over the years that true self-love must be unconditional. If it is not, something will always come up that will make you feel unworthy of your own love. You have to love yourself simply because you exist.

No exceptions. If you tell yourself that you will only love yourself when you are perfect, that day may never come. And a life without self-love is uncomfortable, lonely, and a waste of your many gifts.

In addition to being more likely to succumb to negative self-talk, as a sensitive soul, you will also be more affected by the negative self-talk that you do have. You feel everything deeply so it is easier for you to hurt yourself. Start simply by noticing the words you choose when speaking about yourself. I noticed one day that if I made a mistake, I might mutter phrases like, "I hate myself," or, "How could I be so stupid?" These types of phrases are incredibly potent and only lead to pain and suffering. They need to be eliminated and exchanged for other more kind words. If you are sensitive to what others say about you, you will be even more sensitive to what you say about yourself.

Fill your world with kind, supportive words and thoughts about yourself. When you make a mistake (as we all do), use it as a learning experience and an opportunity to grow rather than as a chance to scold yourself. For example, you could say, "I accept my mistakes and learn from them," or, "I accept myself no matter what." You may find it helpful to imagine treating yourself as you would your own best friend or a young child. Ask yourself, "Would I treat my friend this way?" If not, stop treating yourself that way. Refuse to break your own heart.

It is important to not only work on avoiding negative talk but also on praising yourself for the things that you do well. Once you can learn to be kind and supportive of yourself, you will find that it is easier to love yourself because you will now see yourself as an ally rather than an enemy. You will also be able to love others more fully for who they are without focusing on their faults or being jealous of what they have that you may not have.

Remember, loving yourself does not mean that you have to be perfect. Loving yourself also does not mean that you have to love all of your challenges. For example, if you struggle with anxiety, you don't have to love your anxiety, but you have to love YOU, the person struggling with the anxiety. Your challenges don't define you. Self-love means loving yourself through your challenges and imperfections, understanding that while you may have things you want to improve, you are whole and worthy of love exactly as you are.

You may be thinking right now that unconditional self-love is an impossible task. I can promise you that while it may be challenging to begin with, it is not impossible, and once you are used to it, it will become second nature. You just have to start with self-acceptance, awareness of how you are speaking toward yourself, and continue to practice.

If you are truly committed to the process, slowly but surely, the negative thoughts and words will be replaced by positive ones and you will learn to be on your own side. Remind yourself that you do know how to be loving and compassionate as you are likely a wonderful friend and support system to the people in your life that you love. Now, all you need to do is to apply that love and compassion that comes so easily to you onto yourself. Once you have that, you will not feel alone, because no matter where you go, you will always have one of your best friends and biggest supporters right by your side.

Self-Love Overview

Key Practice Steps:

1. Treat yourself as you would your own best friend or a young child. Accept yourself as you are and love yourself simply because you exist.
2. Avoid speaking harsh words toward yourself, and if you do, replace them with kind words immediately.
3. Forgive yourself for all mistakes, seeing them as opportunities for growth.

What do you love and value about yourself? What are you proud of?

- _____
- _____
- _____

Your Personal Goal: _____

_____

_____

"My beloved child, break your heart no longer. Each time you judge yourself, you break your own heart."

-Swami Kripalu

2

Compassion

Affirmation:
*"I am empathetic, compassionate and kind.
I am understanding of the feelings of others."*

As a sensitive soul, you most likely have a tremendous capacity for compassion and feel empowered when you are able to use your compassionate nature to comfort and nurture others. While you have a strong capacity for compassion, for a variety of reasons, you may not always feel everyone is deserving of your compassion. This can leave you feeling empty. In order to be full of compassion for all those you come into contact with, you must first recognize that you do not know the circumstances of anyone else's life. It is so easy to see someone and judge them based on what you think they should be doing better or to blame them for their actions. However, everyone is doing the best they can with how their brain functions, what they have been taught, their life experiences, and the love (or lack thereof) that they have received in their life. You can never know what it is like to be anyone else but yourself. Living with the understanding that everyone is doing the best they can with what they know allows you to have compassion for all.

When I was in college, I had an internship helping with the faculty at a well-renowned yoga center. There was one highly regarded meditation teacher who was extremely difficult to work with. She was so difficult, in fact, that no one wanted to work directly with her for her upcoming program. Everyone was afraid of her. I decided that this was a perfect opportunity for me to practice my compassion and I volunteered to be her point person. She began by being rude and demanding, but as I continued to remain calm and compassionate toward her, she began to soften as well. By the end of her week-long program, I felt totally comfortable with her and would even consider her kind.

This experience has always stayed with me to remind me the healing power of compassion. I know that it went so well because I was prepared to be compassionate no matter what. If I had come into the situation without that intention, I do not think the week would have worked out so smoothly because I would have likely taken her attitude personally. My sensitive soul would have felt attacked and I would likely have reacted negatively to her demanding nature. I would have later regretted my reaction and likely felt disempowered and overly sensitive. Instead, I ended the week feeling empowered because I was able to embrace my sensitivity and use it as the healing gift that it is.

Start practicing compassion for all those you come in contact with, trust their experience as their own, and allow them to be who they are without judgment. Truly listen to them, regardless of if you agree with their opinion or not. As you learn to listen rather than judge, you will find that your reaction to what is being said will soften, and you will have a better understanding of your fellow human being. Often, what we want more than anything as human beings is just to be heard. When you listen and accept what someone else is feeling, they will feel that acceptance radiating through you. When you allow someone to be who they are, you will also receive the benefit of being at peace within the moment rather than in inner turmoil from fighting what they are feeling. Accept that if you had the same life challenges and experiences they did, that you might feel the same way. Always look to put yourself in someone else's shoes.

There may be people in your life that you have a particularly hard time having compassion for. Maybe a family member comes to mind? Try not to take their actions personally. It is your ego that thinks everything is about you. Everyone's personal journey guides their own actions. For example, if the person at the RMV is rude to you, it is generally not because they have a vendetta against you. Their attitude is not just a reaction to you, but a combination of many things. Maybe it is because the person had a difficult upbringing, is going through a divorce, and hates working at the RMV. Give them the benefit of the doubt. I generally find that those who are the most difficult to deal with are the ones who actually need the most compassion.

Use your interactions with others to practice your compassion and empathy, and to be patient and kind, regardless of how you feel about what they are doing. You will find that this will build an incredible feeling of strength and power, and will most likely set a wonderful example for this person to follow. We may act the way we act because we literally do not know another way. Just because being kind and empathetic is easy for you does not mean it is easy for everyone. When you are able to model compassion for those you come in contact with, your compassion has the ability to spread throughout your community and into the world on a larger scale. Whether we are aware of it or not, we are always learning from one another. Teach with your compassionate heart.

Compassion Overview

Key Practice Steps:

1. Practice compassion toward everyone you meet.

2. Listen first rather than immediately judging. Try to understand where they are coming from.

3. Recognize that those who bother you the most might actually need the most compassion.

Your Personal Goal: _____

_____

_____

_____

_____

_____

_____

"If you want others to be happy,
practice compassion. If you want to be happy,
practice compassion."

-Dalai Lama

3

Trust Yourself

Affirmation:
"I trust myself."

Before you can find your power and place in the world, it is necessary to learn to trust yourself. I have seen many people who have achieved outward success, but were miserable on the inside because they were not being true to themselves and were ignoring that voice in their head telling them to take a different path. Only you can truly know what lights your fire and what you are called to do with your life on this planet. No one else can decide for you.

As a sensitive soul, it is likely that you have a particularly strong connection to your inner wisdom and intuition. Learn to listen to that little voice inside that guides you. You do not always need a logical reason to move forward with something. Simply "knowing" and then following your bliss can be the most powerful action you take. Always move toward what you love.

As an intuitive being, it may be hard to trust yourself because society tells us that we need to have concrete proof of something for it to be meaningful. On a deep level, you know this is not the case and have likely had many experiences to tell you otherwise, but it can be hard to put aside the beliefs of the culture. For me, personally, I have a strong sense of intuition, but I used to second guess it out of fear of making a mistake. If I became overly emotional about a choice, it would be nearly impossible to access my inner wisdom.

The only way to begin to trust yourself is to make a decision when you are relaxed, and then move forward, even if you are not one hundred percent sure if it is the best choice. If you wait to be certain of your choice, then you will not live your fullest life because the day that you finally feel sure of your decision may either never arrive or it may simply be too late. Indecision actually manifests as a decision to stay stuck where you are.

To be successful, you need to take action and move forward, even if you do not know exactly how. If you continuously take small steps, one of them will eventually lead to where you want to go. Even if your voice trembles, hold your head high, speak your truth, and trust what you know to be true for yourself. You simply cannot get anywhere if you freeze or give up when you are unsure. You will either find success or learn something valuable from the experience. The fear of moving forward is almost always worse than any outcome. Think back on the decisions you have made in your life and recognize that all you can do is make the decision that feels right in the moment and trust that it will work out. Keep in mind that there are also usually many right decisions, not just one, and that many decisions can effectively be undone if necessary. Either way, you will always learn something.

For most of my life, I have had difficulty making decisions. I could clearly and effectively help someone else make a decision, but when it came to my own life, I would overthink it. For me, taking time to write how I am feeling in a journal provides me with an outlet to really speak to myself and to look at the big picture as well as to quiet my internal critic. I also enjoy speaking to myself as though I was my own friend or client. When I imagine I am talking to someone else, I end up knowing exactly what to say and how to move forward with so much less fuss and self-judgment. It feels so liberating to trust yourself.

Are you in the habit of asking everyone for advice about what you should do for fear of making a mistake instead of listening to your own inner wisdom? For one week, practice not asking for any advice. Move through whatever challenges arise (within reason) on your own. Meditate, take a walk, journal, role-play with yourself, or sleep on any decisions that feel difficult to you. Over analysis can keep you stuck, so be sure to spend time relaxing and not thinking about your choice. You may find that the less you actively think about it and the more you are able to let your inner wisdom guide you, the easier it will be to come to the right answer for you. As you practice trusting yourself first, your confidence will build, and sooner or later, trusting yourself will become natural.

Trust Yourself Overview

Key Practice Steps:

1. Learn to listen to and trust your inner wisdom.

2. When you need to make a difficult decision, relax and imagine the advice you would give to a friend in your position.

3. Practice trusting yourself first before asking for help.

Your Personal Goal: _____

_____

_____

_____

_____

_____

_____

"As soon as you trust yourself,
then you will know how to live."

-Goethe

4

Express Your Feelings

Affirmation:

"I am willing to express my feelings. As I allow myself to feel my feelings, I am able to let them go."

As a sensitive soul, you have likely been told many times that you should "not feel that way" or to "stop being so sensitive." While you can certainly empower yourself to not take the little things so deeply to heart (more on this in the Mind section), there is a point where not feeling your true feelings is actually extremely detrimental. When you don't allow yourself to feel your feelings, you create resistance in your body, heart, and mind. It is well known that what we resist persists. Resisting how you feel may lead you to consequently ruminate over something much longer than you truly need to. It is generally the resistance to our feelings that causes us the most pain. As you learn to feel your feelings, you train yourself to both respond to them appropriately and to adapt more easily to different scenarios. If you are able to allow your feelings to be what they are without judgment, you create the opportunity for the feelings to pass with grace rather than struggle.

There are many ways to help you express your feelings. One of my favorite ways is through journaling. As I have mentioned before, I find I have better access to my inner wisdom when I journal and can really see a situation for what it is without judgment around it. If you like to write, I highly recommend journaling about your feelings. It can help you sort through them and figure out which ones are important to let go of and what needs to be worked through more deeply.

One of the most essential ways to express your feelings is to speak to someone who you trust and who understands your sensitivity. As a sensitive soul, you likely prefer having a few close friendships rather than a large group of more peripheral friends. It is quite important for you to have a trusted friend who is a good listener and who shows compassion well. Your friend's role is not necessarily to help you fix your problem, rather to listen to you with love and compassion and to help you feel heard. Often, just having someone listen to you is enough to let your feelings go.

That being said, sometimes the best decision is to speak with a professional. A professional could be a coach, counselor, therapist, mentor, teacher, or other form of healer. This person has training to help support you in working through your feelings, and it may be easier for you to fully open up to them because they are not directly involved in your life. It is not a sign of weakness to seek professional help. I believe it is a sign of strength and self-love. Just make sure that the person you choose is someone who you resonate with and who will not be judgmental of you. If the first person you find isn't the right fit, don't give up. Keep looking.

There are many other practices that you could consider using to help you express your feelings including singing, dancing, movement with the intention of letting go of emotion, emotional freedom techniques, and more. I encourage you to explore and see how you feel while practicing these types of techniques.

Pay extra attention to strong feelings such as grief, anger, and fear. If the feelings you experience are so traumatic that you repress them, this can create long-term imbalance in your overall wellbeing. When we don't allow these feelings to surface, they literally and metaphorically get "stuck" in the body, causing unwanted symptoms, pain, and suffering. You may think you are fine for a long period of time, but if the feeling has not been dealt with then it may pop up in the disguise of an illness.

This emotional repression can create immense difficulty in healing the issue because there is no obvious medical cause. I believe this is part of why Western medicine has not proven to be an effective cure for many ailments, but rather more of a Band-Aid. Physical issues are generally addressed (usually with medication) using studies of other people with similar conditions. This can certainly help yield results, but what unfortunately happens is that emotional and individual life circumstances are often not even considered important when figuring out the best remedy. I believe it is absolutely crucial to consider each person's unique issues and emotional needs to achieve comprehensive wellbeing. If you feel you may be repressing deep emotional wounds, I encourage you to seek professional help from someone with a holistic approach who understands the physical effects that unhealed trauma can have on you. The sooner you seek help, the less of a chance that your repressed emotion will create an illness.

I have been lucky to find an amazing doctor/healer for myself who has a seasoned background in Western medicine, augmented with a healthy respect for alternative methods. Most importantly, the way he heals me is specific to me and my own individual issues. I have never felt such care from a doctor as I feel I have now. It might not be easy for you to find your own holistically minded doctor, however, I firmly believe the end result is worth the search.

Are there any unwanted symptoms you are dealing with that you have not been able to pinpoint a physical cause for? Take a moment to scan your body and think of a symptom. Then, using your strong intuition, take some time to ask yourself the true causes of these feelings. What are they trying to tell you? Where are they asking you to grow? What are they asking you to let go of?

Our hardest times always end up being our biggest teachers. If you do not allow yourself to go through your painful feelings, not only will they strengthen, but you will also be cutting off your opportunity for growth. It is okay to break down sometimes. The light at the end of the tunnel is a breakthrough.

Express Your Feelings Overview

Key Practice Steps:

1. Allow yourself to feel your feelings rather than resist them.

2. Practice using journaling as a way to express your feelings and connect to your inner wisdom. Ask yourself, what are my feelings telling me?

3. Speak to a trusted friend or professional as needed and explore other ways of emotional expression.

Your Personal Goal: _____

_____

_____

_____

_____

_____

"The more you hide your feelings,
the more they show. The more you
deny your feelings, the more they grow."

-Author Unknown

5

Prioritize Yourself

Affirmation:
*"I set healthy boundaries for myself.
I stand up for what I need."*

Being sensitive, you may find that your ability to sympathize with someone causes you to say "yes" to something that you may not want or need to do. You may also have a strong fear of disappointing that person by not complying with their wishes. Your initial reaction may be to say "no" but then you overthink it and end up saying "yes" out of guilt or fear of standing up for yourself. If you end up always saying "yes" to other people, what it really means is that you are saying "no" to yourself.

When you know you are not happy to do something, stick to that resolution. Doing something out of guilt will be incredibly draining and unfulfilling, not only for you, but potentially even for the person you are saying yes to. If you are showing even slight signs of bitterness or guilt for saying yes, that person will likely feel it. You would not want someone to do something for you out of guilt, so why would you want to do something for someone else out of guilt?

As a yoga teacher, it is common to get asked quite regularly to cover other teacher's classes. For the first studios I worked for, I felt a strange obligation to cover whenever anyone needed help. I would frequently say "yes" even if it would be a tight fit for me to get to my next session or if it would cause me to cancel my plans. I found myself always regretting the decision to put my needs aside and I'd blame myself for not taking more time to think about it. I knew something needed to change when a couple of years into my teaching career the owner of one of the yoga studios I taught at called to ask if I could cover a class that evening for a teacher who was sick. That day happened to be the two-year anniversary of dating my boyfriend (now fiancé), so at first, I said that I could not cover the class because I had plans for our anniversary. Before hanging up on the call, I started to feel guilty for saying no, and out of my need to please the owner, I changed my mind and said I could teach the class. This ended up being a powerful lesson for me because not only did I have to cancel our special plans, I felt bitter while teaching the class and exhausted when I got home. I made an internal pact with myself to not let my fear of disappointing others cloud my judgment of what I should or should not do, and that has been an incredible (and reasonably simple) life-changing decision for me ever since. It is great to help others, but not at your own continued expense. I know what my priorities are now, and I have learned to not go past my limit and to trust myself to make the decision that is right for me.

Is there something that you regularly agree to do that you would really rather not do? Saying no in these types of situations can be really hard, especially at first, but it is worth it. You will not regret skipping that extra meeting or missing the party you weren't interested in attending in the first place. In fact, you will be pleased with yourself for preserving your energy. When you know something is not right for you, follow the rule of the "quick no" by saying "no" immediately, and then letting it go. Otherwise, you will waste the time and energy of both you and the person who is reaching out to you. Saying no quickly is far more graceful than stringing someone along with something vague or non-committal. When in real doubt of what to do, follow the rule of the "slow yes" by not committing right away. Get more information if you need to and take a night or two to sleep on it. You will then be able to decide through your power rather than through a need to please others.

Prioritize Yourself Overview

Key Practice Steps:

1. Take care of yourself by saying no more regularly.
2. Wait to commit to something until you have thought it through.
3. Say no right away if you do not want to do something.

Your Personal Goal: _____

_____

_____

_____

_____

_____

_____

"I'm not saying no to you;
I am saying yes to me."

-Priti Robyn Ross

6

Appreciation

Affirmation:

"I observe and appreciate the countless blessings in my life each and every day."

Do you ever feel frustrated with yourself because you have many positive aspects of your life but you tend to spend most of your energy thinking about the areas that are not going as well? This is actually quite predictable. It is evolutionarily hard-wired in us to deal with what we see as a problem before we focus on anything else. Our modern brains still respond to stress in the same way they did when we needed to run away from lions to protect ourselves, so it makes sense that our brains try to focus on our problems so that we can survive. The problem is that our brains do not realize that the things we tend to stress over are actually rarely related to our immediate survival and are often not particularly important. Luckily, since day-to-day survival is not what so many of us struggle with, we have the opportunity to train our brains for grateful living.

As a sensitive soul, you have a strong capacity to see and feel the immense suffering in life as well as to enjoy life's beauty and blessings. You can use appreciation to help illuminate the positive aspects in your life as well as to let go of unnecessary suffering. Due to your sensitive nature, you are likely to be even more positively impacted by undergoing a gratitude practice than most. Each time you notice yourself worrying about something or complaining, immediately think of something you are grateful for and notice how that softens your worry.

Ask yourself, "What is there to appreciate in this moment?" As you answer, feel the sense of ease and clarity flood back into you. I find it helpful to speak your gratitude out loud, affirming to yourself and the universe that you are appreciative of the blessings in your life.

Many sensitive souls benefit from a more formal practice such as a daily gratitude journal. For example, before you go to bed each day, you might practice gratitude by writing five or ten experiences you are grateful for from the day. You might wake up in the morning and say, "I am grateful for this new day," or something along those lines that resonates with you. You can practice thanking those in your life for everything they do for you. Your body and mind will respond positively to true appreciation, as will those around you who you start remembering to thank. It is truly a win-win mindset. Another practice that I enjoy is simply writing down your favorite moment of each day. You can then look back on all the wonderful moments you had all at once to be reminded of the beauty in your life.

I also find it helpful to focus on appreciation for the people in your life with whom you have difficulty with. Especially in a challenging relationship, we can tend to focus too much attention on what we don't like about someone without taking enough time to appreciate his or her gifts. Next time you find yourself thinking of someone's negative qualities, immediately find a moment of appreciation for their positive ones. You will find that even in your most difficult relationships there are many things to appreciate about the other person. This new perspective may even have the power to turn an enemy into a friend, for as you soften your feelings toward others, it is likely that their feelings will soften toward you.

To fully experience a life of gratitude, it is equally important to be appreciative for the simple things in life as well as the obvious larger blessings. I was reminded of this recently when I participated in a twenty-one-day course led by entrepreneur and author, Kate Northrup. The exercise for day fourteen was to write down everything you had received that day including gifts, compliments, helpful feedback, kind gestures, lessons, etc. I hadn't had the best day and I sat down to write out what I had received before bed, thinking I had not received very much that day. To my surprise, once I started writing, I could not stop. I thought of over twenty gifts I received that day (most of which came in the form of help or kind gestures) and I could have kept going. I fell asleep feeling so much more appreciative and full than I normally do because I had taken the time to focus on the positive rather than the negative. We have the power to cultivate this sense of appreciation every single day if we remember to count the little blessings in our lives.

It is also important to watch the words you use in regards to your life. Avoid using phrases like, "My life sucks," or, "I never win." These kinds of phrases will only foster the energy that you do not want in your life. Instead, think or say something such as, "My life is full of beauty," or, "I appreciate each new opportunity and experience in my life." This is a simple practice with profound implications. Affirm your appreciation every single day and you will be amazed how it changes the way you experience your life. With appreciation, a feeling of fear and lack of resources will be replaced with a feeling of positivity and abundance.

Appreciation Overview

Key Practice Steps:

1. Experiment with an appreciation practice such as gratitude journaling or speaking gratitude in times of struggle.

2. Speak only gracious words about your life.

3. Thank someone each and every day for the gifts they bring you.

Your Personal Goal: _____

_____

_____

_____

_____

_____

"Gratitude unlocks the fullness of life. It turns what we have into enough and more. It turns denial into acceptance, chaos to order, confusion to clarity. It can turn a meal into a feast, a house into a home, a stranger into a friend."

-Melody Beatti

7

Accept Constructive Criticism

Affirmation:
"I accept criticism with an open mind."

As a sensitive person, even gentle criticism can feel like an almost unbearable attack on your soul, and that what is being said holds no constructive value because the person is just being mean. This is especially true if you have not yet learned to love yourself unconditionally. If that is the case, you likely have a strong tendency to recoil in the face of criticism to protect yourself. You may also bounce the criticism back to the person who gave it you to, immediately reacting in a negative way. This is understandable because if you are constantly criticizing yourself, it simply hurts too much to hear any more criticism than what you are already giving yourself.

I have been extremely sensitive to criticism ever since I can remember. In early elementary school, I earned high marks in all areas on my report cards except for "Accepts Constructive Criticism." I still remember that because it hurt my feelings to be criticized for not taking criticism well! I had one teacher in third grade even tell me that the only reason she put me in the advanced reading group is because she thought I would have taken it too personally if I was not included. So if you have trouble with criticism, I can empathize. This has been a constant theme throughout my adult life as well.

While there can certainly be pain attached with criticism, there is simultaneously tremendous opportunity for growth. We are here on this planet to grow and evolve as human beings, and each day is another step on that path. Through feedback and criticism, particularly if it is spoken with love, we can grow faster, as others can often see where we are limited more than we can. It is impossible to go through life without criticism, so you may as well learn to use it to your advantage. Instead of seeing criticism as another bullet point on your list of why you are not good enough, see it as an opportunity to grow.

Once I was able to shift my mindset and recognize that I have learned many valuable insights through criticism, I began to see criticism as generally helpful rather than hurtful. I am still a little weary of it, but as I hold the right intention, it gets easier each time. It is essential to realize that not all critical comments come from someone wanting to hurt you. More likely, the person actually wants to help you. They just may not give their critique in the nicest way or in a way that you can effectively hear it. To help you become more comfortable, I recommend that you occasionally ask for constructive criticism from someone that you trust and know will be gentle with your sensitive heart. That way, you will feel more in control of the situation because it is on your terms with someone you respect. You can then learn from the feedback rather than getting caught up in being upset by it.

With each critical comment you receive in the world, take a moment, or even a day or two, to breathe and digest what is being said. Taking this time will allow you to have a greater understanding of what was said without as much interference from your emotional reaction to it. From there, you can move forward with what truly resonates with you and leave what does not. Without pausing first, you may notice that you are actually most reactive to those comments that are true. Again, the key is to love yourself through the moment, to know that your value in life does not come from being perfect. It is truly empowering to listen to criticism without feeling any less worthy as a human being. If you feel you have work to do on self-love, start there first, and then focus on accepting criticism when you are more unconditionally supportive of yourself.

Accept Constructive Criticism Overview

Key Practice Steps:

1. Listen to constructive criticism with an open mind.

2. Take time to breathe and think about what was said before reacting.

3. Take what is helpful for your growth and let go of the rest.

Your Personal Goal: _____

_____

_____

_____

_____

_____

_____

"Praise makes you feel good.
Criticism makes you better."

-Author Unknown

8

Forgiveness

Affirmation:

"I am willing to forgive myself.
I am willing to forgive others."

As a sensitive soul, you likely experience more pain and suffering than most. You may also be more likely to hold onto your pain rather than letting it go. You are likely quite sensitive to the needs of others, so you may struggle to understand how some people can seem so insensitive at times. It is helpful to remember that most people are likely not as skilled at compassion and empathy as you are, and may actually be unable to see the situation from your perspective or understand your feelings no matter how obvious you might think it seems. Even if they desire to, they may not be able to treat you as kindly as you are able to treat them.

When there are people in our lives that we have not forgiven, it keeps us stuck in the past, bonded to old pain and suffering. Many people hesitate to forgive because they think that forgiving someone means that you are somehow validating what the person did. This is not the case. Forgiveness does not condone what happened. It is simply an attitude of acceptance and letting go so that you can move forward. Something terrible may have happened, but you learn to accept the situation because anything other than acceptance is fighting against reality, and you cannot win when you fight reality.

It can be helpful to write a journal entry imagining

the situation from the other person's perspective. You may see aspects in a new light that help to soften your emotions around what happened. Assuming that a person is doing the best they can is incredibly beneficial and empowering, even if someone's best appears quite subpar to you. When you do not allow yourself to forgive, you are doing yourself a disservice, choosing to embrace negativity rather than compassion and understanding. We cannot truly know what it is like to be someone else or know the past difficulties that others have gone through. Every terrible act that anyone has committed stems from his or her own pain and suffering. If we have compassion and forgiveness, we can learn to let go of the past and set ourselves free.

Being a sensitive soul, I used to be easily hurt by friends and family members. I also tended to hold onto those feelings of hurt and to let some of my friendships end because I could not let go of the past. Over the last few years, I spent many evenings writing in my journal about forgiveness, taking time to see each situation that was still painful to me from the other person's perspective. This helped me to let go of the negativity I was harboring and move on. I would light a candle, say a forgiveness affirmation, and exhale away any grudge I was holding because I knew it was what I needed to do to heal. In most cases, I was struck with the realization that the person was doing what they thought was best at the time and that they did not mean to cause me any harm. If you have people in your life to forgive, I recommend you try the journaling exercise, forgiveness affirmations, or even to write the person a letter that you never send.

A meaningful distinction here is that forgiveness is for you, not necessarily for the other person. This may mean choosing to no longer have contact or a relationship with someone who has hurt you, but that you do not harbor negativity toward them in your heart. In order to heal, sometimes you need to let go of relationships that are unhealthy.

It is also fundamental to learn to forgive yourself. We look back at our past mistakes from our current point of view and think we should have known better, but you cannot judge yourself now on what you did not know in the past. You were doing the best you could. Hindsight is 20/20. That is a good thing. It means you have learned from your mistakes. Now it is time to forgive yourself and others so that you can live fully in the present rather than being held back by the past. It is a brave and empowering act to forgive and you will be rewarded with a weight lifted off your shoulders and more peace in your heart.

Forgiveness Overview

Key Practice Steps:

1. Practice forgiving those who hurt you in the past, including yourself. Assume the person was doing the best they could.

2. Understand that forgiveness is to help you. You do not need to continue a relationship with that person.

3. Periodically check in with yourself to see if there is anyone who you need to forgive. Write them a note you do not send or meditate on forgiving them. Let it go.

Your Personal Goal: _____

_____

_____

_____

_____

_____

"To forgive is to set a prisoner free and discover that the prisoner was you."

-Lewis B. Smedes

9

Eliminate Negative Comparisons

Affirmation:

"I am inspired by the strengths I see in others."

Everyone treats comparison uniquely. For many, the act of comparing oneself to another will either lead to actionable motivation or debilitating discouragement. Comparison can be inspiring and educational when approached with an open mind, but extremely deflating if viewed from a perspective of self-doubt. As a sensitive soul, you may look at what other people are doing and think, "Oh, she is so much better than me," or, "Wow, I could never be like that." To do this is to devalue your own sense of self-worth, instilling an obligation within you to be someone you are not. You will not be satisfied or feel whole if you are always wishing to be more like someone else. You are the only you in the whole world, and your work is to become the best you and no one else.

Instead of comparing yourself to others for the purpose of focusing on your faults, practice looking to others for inspiration. Recognize the qualities you admire and be grateful that someone is modeling those qualities for you to learn from. Allow the success of those around you to uplift you, to inspire you, and to make you stronger rather than make you feel empty. We all have different strengths and weaknesses. You cannot be someone else, but you can work to be the best you.

As a sensitive soul, you likely have perfectionist tendencies. This is something I have struggled with a lot. Before I started teaching yoga, I remember being intimidated by all of the other yoga teachers. I thought what they were doing was highly impressive and that it was beyond my abilities to be like them. However, to my own pleasant surprise, as I practiced and improved, I continued to become as skilled as the teachers I had looked up to. Even so, once I got to that level, I found myself still unsatisfied because my bar for what a "great teacher" was became so high that even though the younger me would have been impressed with my evolved skillset, the current me still felt inadequate because I saw there was so much more to learn. This is when I learned a fundamental truth that as humans there is always more we can do to better ourselves.

No matter who you are or what you know, we all have something to learn and the ability to improve. The sooner you can accept that, the sooner you can appreciate all that you do have to offer. Seek to value what you already know and yearn to add to that foundation that is already within you. When I learned to look at these exact same teachers as pure inspiration rather than a reason to feel disempowered, my feelings completely changed and there was no longer a problem at all. I looked at them as mentors to help me evolve my own skills instead of as opportunities to find shortcomings within my work. You must see the strengths of others as a way to be uplifted rather than a reason to make you feel like you are not good enough. There is always someone who knows more than you and that is okay. Consider yourself lucky to have someone to help you grow. How uninspiring would life be if you were already better than everyone at everything and there was nothing left to learn?

Have you ever met someone and immediately disliked him or her because they were strong in one area where you were not? Maybe they were extremely outgoing or bold and that made you feel your sensitivity was a weakness. When seeing the strengths of others, it is important to make sure that you are not suffering from unconscious (or conscious) jealousy. It is human nature to unfairly dislike someone because they have something that you wish you had. This is a way to deflect poor self-esteem, because for many people, it is easier to feel jealous than to feel like you are not good enough. If you feel good about yourself, seeing someone else succeed will make you feel good too. Notice the tendency to judge people for their strengths. If you find yourself doing this, take a deep breath and instead think of a compliment you could give them and also a compliment to give yourself. Learn to appreciate someone else's gifts without questioning your own.

Due to social media and our cultural fascination with celebrities, we tend to have a warped sense of how successful and happy other people are. It is like we are looking at someone's life highlight reel and comparing it to the normal ups and downs of our day-to-day lives. If you are not mindful of this, it can easily make you feel unworthy. The truth is that many of the most "successful" people are the least happy and feel the worst about themselves. I briefly worked with a celebrity client and he was easily one of the most unbalanced and anxious people I have ever worked with. Make sure to keep that in perspective as you make assumptions based on highlight reels.

Even while keeping this in mind, it is easy to still feel disempowered when you see someone who you feel a sense of jealously toward. Instead, try to watch how this person moves through the world. Take note of their strengths. Depending on who they are, consider reaching out to them to connect or even break through the jealousy and give them a compliment! Use this as a learning experience rather than an opportunity to beat yourself up. The goal is not to end up being just like him or her, but instead to be inspired to make a few slight changes that help you feel more empowered in the world. You do not have to wait to find a perfect role model to do this with either. It is okay to find someone who has some qualities you view as negative, but also has a few special qualities that you would love to cultivate. No one is perfect. Learn from what resonates with you, let go of what does not, and remember that you are not trying to be anyone else. You are working to be the most empowered version of yourself. No matter what, always be kind to yourself as you learn.

Eliminate Negative Comparisons Overview

Key Practice Steps:

1. Allow the positive qualities in others to inspire you.

2. Let go of any feelings of unworthiness for not being like someone else and avoid negative comparison.

3. Work toward being the best you.

Your Personal Goal: _____

_____

_____

_____

_____

_____

_____

"Comparison is the thief of joy."

-Theodore Roosevelt

10

Protect Your Energy

Affirmation:
*"I release all energy that is not
of my highest and best interest."*

We are all give off energy, and every interaction with someone is an exchange of that energy. Think of the term, "Laughing is contagious." Most of us have felt it—that feeling when you're being overwhelmed by someone else's positive energy and you react to it involuntarily. As a sensitive soul, you likely have highly receptive empathic tendencies and may frequently pick up on energy from a person or group who is having a strong emotion. Sometimes this can be nice, as with the laughter example, but many times, the strong emotion is a negative one. For example, if you are feeling great, but walk into a meeting with someone who is deeply upset, you will likely have your happy mood dampened. Even if you remain compassionate and calm, it may not be enough to protect you from the suffering of others. It is necessary to create a protection around you so that you can hold onto your power and not create any unwanted feelings within you.

You may have had the experience in a crowd or group setting of attaching to the negative feelings of others without realizing it. Maybe you were in a social setting and you started to feel negativity for no known reason. During these times, it is very helpful to first ask yourself, "What am I feeling?" and, "Do I have this feeling for a specific reason?" Chances are likely that if the feeling came on suddenly, out of nowhere, and you can't think of why you would feel that way, then you may have unknowingly taken on someone else's energy. Once you recognize that the feeling does not belong to you, you will likely be able to relax around it more and then you can work on protecting your energy. Even just naming the feeling can help you separate from it.

By creating the intention to protect your energy, you can start to build the defense that you need to stay strong in the midst of negativity. My favorite way to protect my energy is to say out loud (or in my head if it cannot be said out loud), "I release all energy that is not of my highest and best interest." When you are in a situation where you feel your vitality being weakened, repeat this phrase multiple times in a row while taking deep breaths and imagining all negative energy leaving your body. Keep your presence on your body, your breath, and the feeling of peace that is deep inside of your body no matter what is going on with someone else. The more in your body you can stay, the less likely their energy will affect you.

This was a necessary lesson for me to learn as a yoga teacher. When I began teaching group classes years ago, I usually felt strong during class, but would frequently feel strangely drained of energy and discouraged afterward. I recognized that I was not creating enough of a boundary between the students and myself. This was important because with a class full of people, it is likely that at least one of them is going through something emotionally intense and palpable. Now I pay extra attention to centering myself before, during, and after my class. I repeat my affirmation and feel stronger and more balanced after I teach. I also found that having physical contact with too many students was draining for me, and it is best for me to cue with words more often than with hands on adjustments. If you are in a healing arts profession, you likely need to take even more care to release your client's energy.

You may find that you need to rest after being in front of a group or in a social setting. Let yourself have the rest you need and be careful not to schedule too many activities in one day. If there is someone in your life that you suspect may be draining you, specifically affirm that you release their energy and pain from your body. There may be people in your life who you need to let go of or at least limit your interaction with. That is okay. Know that your sensitivity is a gift and that while you may feel more negative energy, you will also be able to feel positive energy too.

Another important part of protecting your energy is to work on not being overly upset by the little annoyances in life. We will discuss this more in the Mind section, but know that whenever you feel overly emotional, you are likely draining some of your vital energy. You can gain some of your energy back by reconnecting with nature, through going outside, taking deep breaths, or even taking a shower or a bath.

There are also ways that you may be draining (or increasing) your own energy that you may not have thought of. Try to think outside the box. I find rushing, indecision, lack of direction, anxiety, negativity, eating poor quality food, not eating or sleeping enough, talking too fast, too much electricity, and complaining all reduce my energy significantly. On the other hand, I find gratitude, compassion, positivity, socializing with kind people, writing, eating healthy food and helping others all increase my energy. Take note of what activities and mental states increase your energy, which ones drain your energy, and try to adjust accordingly.

Protect Your
Energy Overview

Key Practice Steps:

1. Bring awareness to what increases your energy and what drains your energy.

2. Practice your protection affirmation when you feel your energy being drained.

3. Keep your presence on yourself and your body when speaking with someone in distress, maintaining a sense of strength and separateness.

What increases your energy?

- _____

- _____

- _____

What drains your energy?

- _____

- _____

- _____

Your Personal Goal: _____

_____

_____

_____

_____

_____

_____

"Energy is contagious, positive and negative alike.
I will forever be mindful of what and who I am
allowing into my space."

-Alex Elle

11

Choose Love

Affirmation:
"My heart is open. I love freely."

As a sensitive soul who has been hurt a lot, I spent many years living with my heart not fully open. I was afraid of being hurt again. I was afraid that if I offered my love, I might not get it back and would be left empty. Can you relate? This is not a good strategy because you rarely get what you want if you do not send it out first. You have to take the first step and give love to the world without any expectation of return. When you are able to do that, you realize that choosing love is for you as much as it is for whomever you are sending that love to. You are actually receiving love by giving it.

When you meet someone, is your attitude one of welcoming and love or of judgment and criticism? Are you sizing the other person up or are you genuinely curious to get to know them? Are you concerned with getting your needs met or are you curious about how you can help and serve others? Just going into an interaction with the intention to send loving energy toward someone can soften tension and create ease in just about any situation.

I used to be very shy and anxious when I was younger, especially in social situations. Looking back, I realize that the people I met likely interpreted my shy, anxious nature as unfriendliness. I'm still fairly shy in a large social setting, but now that I feel more empowered in my sensitive soul, I have recognized that people respond well to my kind, compassionate yet introverted nature. It is now easier for me to be myself in a group because I am coming from a place of love and openness rather than fear. I know that when I am true to myself and speak and act from a place of love that I will be well received. If I'm not well received, then I don't take it personally anymore because I know I have done my best.

If deciding to send out more love seems daunting, there are many ways to begin to open your heart, including the topics we have already discussed such as self-acceptance, trusting yourself, gratitude, compassion, and forgiveness. The more comfortable you feel in your own skin, the easier it is to love. There are also more specific practices that help you connect with your literal heart. I like setting a daily intention. I wake up in the morning and place my hands on my heart and set the intention to meet each person I see with love and acceptance. I also recommend checking in with your heart periodically throughout the day. When you notice yourself feeling negativity or reacting poorly to a situation, bring your attention to your heart. Hold your heart again and breathe into it. Send healing energy to yourself. I also recommend practicing heart opening yoga poses to literally and metaphorically open your heart, especially restorative backbends. Make sure your daily standing and sitting posture is strong so you are not rounding your back and physically guarding your heart. Stay aware of your breath. As you slow down your breath, you will also relax your heart.

If you feel your heart is closed, continue to practice opening your heart every day until it becomes natural. Make sure that you are also sending love to yourself. You need to love yourself in order to freely give your love to others.

Remember to always tell your loved ones that you love them. Hug your friends and family tightly and let them truly feel the love you have for them. Smile at strangers, be kind and compassionate to all, and your heart will fill with love. Your love will be infectious and you will find that you attract more kindhearted people into your life. Each moment holds the potential for pure love if you allow it to.

Choose Love Overview

Key Practice Steps:

1. When in doubt, let love guide you.

2. Practice unconditional love for yourself and all beings.

3. If you feel your heart is closed, sit up tall, place your hands on your heart, breathe deeply, and repeat your affirmation.

Your Personal Goal: _____

_____

_____

_____

_____

_____

_____

"Love is the bridge between
you and everything."

-Rumi

12

Ways to Find Balance

Affirmation:
*"When I feel out of balance,
I know just what to do to reset myself."*

As a sensitive soul, you may regularly have times when you find yourself feeling emotionally out of balance. You may feel anxious, depressed, fatigued, overwhelmed, or even out of control. In those unsteady moments, it is easy to spiral into feelings of helplessness and want to give up. However, in those exact moments, you also have an opportunity to care of yourself deeply and intentionally choose to take time to reset yourself.

To do this easily and effectively, it is helpful to have a go-to list of practices you can do to regain peace and perspective. For me, there is nothing that compares to a nap. When I feel overwhelmed, tired, anxious, or out of balance (and I have time), I always know I can retreat into bed and rest from the busy world around me. As a sensitive soul, you may feel the same need. I wasted a lot of time feeling bad about this and thinking it made me weak, but as I embrace my need for and love of naps, I recognize the true healing power they have for me, and how wonderful it is that I have something to go to that helps me so much. Naps do not make me weak, they make me strong because I feel so much more able to handle anything that comes my way when I wake up. I also love getting outside, especially being in the sunshine, and of course, practicing yoga always has a way of positively shifting my mood. What works best for you?

Below are some of my suggestions for how to regain your sense of balance and peace in your heart. Take some from my list or create your own. Keep your list close to you so that when you are not feeling well, you can go directly to the list and pick what feels doable to you in that moment.

My Favorite Ways to Find Balance

Yoga, meditation, journaling, taking a long shower or a bath, deep breathing, calling a friend, watching a funny movie, singing, listening to music, dancing, running, taking a walk, reading an inspirational book, repeating positive affirmations, tai chi, art projects, listening to a comedian, cooking, lying in the grass, dry body brushing, writing down what you are grateful for, getting dressed up, getting into your pajamas, playing with a pet, taking a nap, walking in the woods, sitting in the sun, saying no to activities you do not want to do, throwing away clutter, asking for help, coloring, walking with your feet in the grass, swimming, stretching, singing, dancing.

Ways to Find Balance Overview

Key Practice Steps:

1. Create a list of your favorite activities to help you when you feel out of balance.

2. Refer to the list when you are not feeling your best, pick an activity, and do it without judging yourself for it.

3. Be extra kind to yourself when you aren't feeling well. This is when you need your own support the most.

Activities that help you find balance:

- _____

- _____

- _____

Your Personal Goal: _____

_____

_____

_____

"I have come to believe that caring for myself is not self-indulgent. Caring for myself is an act of survival."

-Audre Lorde

PART 3

Mind

Affirmation:
*"I am smart, confident, and strong.
I have the power to create a positive outlook."*

Your mindset colors everything you do, every decision you make, every day of your life. I saved mindset for the last section because I see it as the place with the most opportunity for growth. Once you are able to move into an empowered, positive mindset, the world is your oyster and your entire life becomes easier. While this is the most significant section, it can also be the hardest and may take the most work. We all agree that we need to practice to become skilled at something, so why should mindset training be any different? Remember that powerful change takes time, patience, and practice. As you read the next section, avoid making any judgments or limiting your ability to succeed at changing your mindset. Your mind may try to tell you it is not possible because you may have not done it before. That is a mind trick that keeps you stuck. Open your mind, body, and heart to your own power and you will be rewarded immensely. You can do anything you set your mind to.

1

Choose a Positive Outlook

Affirmation:
*"My true nature is happiness, joy, and love.
I radiate positive energy."*

I find that it is common to believe that your mindset is set in stone and that your outlook on life cannot be changed. I believe that this way of thinking is often an excuse to stay stuck where you are and to not take control over your life. In order to have a positive life, it is fundamentally important to work on cultivating a positive mindset. If you feel like you could use a more positive outlook, this step starts with first accepting any negativity within you and then bringing awareness to it. When you notice you are being unnecessarily negative, simply say, "Oops," or as one of my yoga teachers, Judith Hanson Lasater, would say, "How human of me," and then reframe the situation. Accepting unnecessary negativity is actually incredibly liberating as it means you are taking an honest look at yourself and choosing to take control over your life.

One reason why you might get stuck in a negative mindset is due to an over-identification with your thoughts. Each and every day, thousands of thoughts are flowing in and out of your mind, but that doesn't mean that those thoughts represent you or that they even resonate with who you are as a person and your values. With training and practice, you can recognize that you have power in the moment to take or leave any thought that comes to your mind.

As a sensitive soul, I have always experienced my feelings

deeply. As a child, I had a constant and insatiable desire for love and affection. I also unconsciously recognized that I would get attention and love from having a problem. This instinctively created a pattern of negativity and suffering in me. Instead of looking on the bright side, I focused on and verbalized everything that was wrong. If I felt like my feelings were not understood or taken seriously I would often slightly exaggerate them to get my point across so that hopefully I could get the affection I was looking for. It took me years to recognize and accept that my negative outlook was cultivated internally and greatly affecting my health and happiness. At first, it was very painful to see myself in that light; so painful that I did not want to accept it. However, once I was able to accept this with an attitude of self-love and work to change my patterns of negativity, it was the most liberating step I have ever taken. Through taking control of my mindset, I realized that I had much more power than I thought I did and that this negativity was not the real me. It was just a symptom that had been deeply ingrained in me over time.

To start the process of moving into a more positive and empowering mindset, begin by limiting complaining and gossiping or any unconscious embellishment of your problems. You may think you enjoy those states because you may get a rush of energy or emotion or attention while in them, however, have you ever noticed how you feel afterward? You will likely feel weak and depleted. When you choose positivity, your life will start to flow more easily and you will be much happier with yourself. You will also start to notice the negativity and pessimism of those around you more easily, and you will be able to remove yourself from situations that bring you down.

When you notice a negative thought, use appreciation to help reframe the situation in your mind, focusing on what is good, what is right, and what is lucky. Truly, the most important step is to create awareness around negativity, and once you do, having a positive mindset will become easier and easier over time. Once you are accustomed to your new outlook, negative thoughts will start to feel so uncomfortable that you will easily remember to reframe your situation. It is expected that you will forget and drop back into unnecessary negativity sometimes, but what is important is working on shortening the time between forgetting and remembering.

Throughout your life, you will most certainly go through hard times and struggles. Sometimes your pain and sadness will be an essential part of your healing journey. In a loving way, you can allow yourself to feel your pain while coming out in the end a stronger version of yourself. Our challenges are always our biggest teachers. When we view them that way, even the most difficult situation can be viewed in a more positive light. If you cannot be happy, then fully allow yourself to be sad rather than fighting yourself for being sad. Resisting your true feelings is actually much more uncomfortable than the feelings themselves. If you allow yourself to feel your feelings, you can much more easily let them go. Use your strong sense of intuition to recognize what is a true feeling that needs to be felt and what is unnecessary. You will likely have no trouble telling the difference.

As a sensitive soul, if you feel that you have work to do in this area, you might consider starting here first. If you learn to be more positive, you will begin to heal and grow in ways you may not have believed were possible. This has been the most empowering change in my life. I was tired of unconsciously choosing pain and negativity, so one day, I decided I would no longer accept that attitude and see what happens. The benefits in my life have been so profound that I would not even be able to go back to the way I was before. I am more relaxed, happy, confident, and loving. I have better relationships, more energy, I am more open-minded, and now value myself in a way I did not think was possible. I am not saying this to brag. I am saying this to tell you with my deepest sincerity that if I can do it, you can do it too.

Choose a Positive Outlook Overview

Key Practice Steps:

1. Limit complaining, gossiping, whining, or unnecessary negativity as much as you can.

2. Notice when you are putting an overly negative spin on a situation and, without judgment, reframe your outlook using more positive words.

3. Focus on the positive aspects of any given person, place, or thing rather than the negative aspects.

Your Personal Goal: _____

_____

_____

_____

_____

_____

_____

"If you change the way you look at things,
the things you look at change."

-Dr. Wayne Dyer

2

Accept What Is

Affirmation:
"I accept this moment."

Simply put, emotional pain and suffering are caused by not accepting the circumstances of the moment. By labeling a situation or experience as good or bad, we immediately create the idea in our minds that something "should" or "should not" be happening. Not wanting what is happening in the moment to be happening creates internal struggle because you are fighting with reality. By learning to accept the moment rather than fight it, you can set yourself free.

It is essential to keep in mind that acceptance of the moment does not mean that you lose your power over your situation or succumb to harmful or destructive actions. It is actually an act of empowerment. Acknowledge the situation and decide if you can take action against what is happening or if you need to remove yourself from the situation altogether. If you find that you cannot change the situation or remove yourself from it, then you work to accept it. These are truly the only empowered options. It is important to note that this may mean accepting that you are sad or hurt by something. If you can accept and allow your feelings, you can more easily move forward from them.

I was taught this lesson of acceptance early in life. I was born with two short fingers and six missing joints in my right hand. While it has certainly made me self-conscious at times, I have not let it get me down. I know that not accepting what I was born with would only cause me tremendous pain because there is nothing I can do about it. It would drain my energy and lower my self-confidence, and for what purpose? There would truly be no purpose at all. If I find myself not being accepting of something frustrating that happens in my day, I remind myself that I know how to accept what is. I have done it before so I can do it again. My energy is precious and I don't want to waste it on something I can't change. You likely have many aspects of your life that you have learned or grown to accept. Use that as proof that you can accept things that cannot be changed too.

To explore this topic more, I recommend Eckhart Tolle's, *The Power of Now*, and Byron Katie's, *Loving What Is*. In order to really ingrain these teachings, you will need to commit to practicing. As you notice your lack of acceptance of the moment, you will begin to see firsthand the pain that your lack of acceptance causes. If you catch yourself not accepting what is, take a deep breath, let your body soften, and repeat your affirmation of acceptance. You will likely then feel a wave of relaxation come over you as you experience the power of allowing the moment to be what it is.

If you are having trouble with that practice, ask yourself these questions: What is the benefit to you holding onto the negative feeling? Is the feeling based in reality or is it fear for something in the future? How would you feel if you let go of that resistance? The more you question and understand the negative feelings you have, the less power they have over you. If you were to do nothing in this book except to learn to accept each moment for what it is, I would consider that a tremendous success.

Accept What Is Overview

Key Practice Steps:

1. Practice acceptance of the moment, exactly as it is.

2. If you cannot accept something, then work to change it or remove yourself from the situation.

3. If something cannot be changed, you cannot remove yourself, and it is difficult to accept, ask yourself what benefit your lack of acceptance is giving you? How would you feel if you let it go?

Your Personal Goal: _____

_____

_____

_____

_____

_____

_____

"Accept–then act. Whatever the present moment contains, accept it as if you had chosen it. This will miraculously transform your whole life."

-Eckhart Tolle

3

Choose Your Words Thoughtfully

Affirmation:
"The words I choose reflect my best intentions."

Our words hold enormous power. They have the ability to completely alter how we feel about a given situation and they can create lasting friendships or cause lifelong feuds. Once spoken, words cannot be taken back, so it is important to speak your words with care and have your words truly reflect your best intentions. As a sensitive soul, you are likely to be very thoughtful with how you speak to others. You are likely aware of other people's feelings and do not want to cause any harm to anyone. We have discussed previously the importance of the words you choose to speak about yourself, so in this section we will focus on how you choose to speak about your life.

Do you ever find yourself unconsciously overemphasizing a negative situation or story to get your point across or for empathy? You may not even realize you are doing this, but it is an unhealthy pattern because your body and mind will start to believe any exaggeration in your story. If you reinforce, for example, "I just had the worst day ever," you will create that sensation in your body, even if it was only a mediocre day, far from the worst day ever. Being honest with yourself requires full honesty in your words. Before you speak, take a breath and really speak from your truth rather than your pain. Your pain will always want to exaggerate its suffering to create more pain and remain present. You have the power to end that cycle by not giving into it and keeping your words in alignment with reality.

The first step to creating a more thoughtful way of speaking is to notice the way you describe your life and how you feel when you do. Notice when you say something overly negative. Do you feel empowered and strong or do you feel weak and vulnerable? Practice putting a positive twist on your words and then feel the internal strength and peace that it builds as you speak from your true self rather than from your pain. This doesn't mean that you can't say that you had a bad day, but it means potentially reframing what qualifies as a bad day. It is also important to accept how you truly feel.

Learning to be more precise with my words helped me in many ways, including helping me to heal from my chronic fatigue. I noticed that if I said, "I feel so tired," or, "I have no energy," that I would feel weakened. Now, when I feel tired, I might say, "I could use a nice nap today," or, "I have all the energy I need today," and this genuinely helps me feel stronger. I am communicating to my body, saying, "It's okay!" instead of, "It's not okay!" You'll notice that using your words with care will help soften anxiety and worry around your situation and help you to feel more empowered and in control. It is a simple technique that can have a profound impact.

My favorite way to practice creating the reality I want is to use positive affirmations. With affirmations, you take the power of language into your own hands to create your life. When practiced consistently, your affirmations will become deeply rooted in your thinking and will flow from you naturally and with ease. If you are tempted to finish this book and not experiment with the affirmations, I understand that it might feel unnatural at first, but please give them a try. You cannot know the true power of something unless you experience it for yourself. Commit to practicing for at least two weeks and then evaluate how you feel. Either way, continue to notice the words you choose to use and to reframe them when they are not truly serving your highest purpose.

Choose Your Words
Thoughtfully Overview

Key Practice Steps:

1. Choose your words with care.

2. If you use words that are overly negative, start over and replace them with more positive words.

3. Practice positive affirmations daily.

Your Personal Goal: _____

_____

_____

_____

_____

_____

_____

"The more you talk about negative things in your life, the more you call them in. Speak victory, not defeat."

- Joel Osteen

4

Respond Rather Than React

Affirmation:
"I respond to difficult situations with integrity."

As a sensitive being, you may have a tendency to react quickly to pain or to an emotion you may feel from a given situation or conversation. You may feel easily attacked and that you need to protect yourself by reacting before taking the time to think over what the true intention was behind what was said. This is a common pattern for many of us, but with awareness and practice, it is easy to break. Thinking before you speak is the pathway to making sure your words align with how you truly feel.

Having been someone who prided myself on being sweet and loving, I was often discouraged by my inability to not react, or "snap," on occasion. Each time it happened, I would recognize almost immediately that I had not thought through my words and had reacted purely from my emotions. This habit made me feel disempowered and lowered my self-esteem. The person I knew I was in my heart wouldn't act that way, so why did it still happen? Once I learned to take a deep breath first, feel the emotion that came up, and then speak from a place of wisdom rather than pain, I felt much more empowered and more aligned with my true self. I learned to respond instead of react.

It is helpful to recognize that there is often a deeply ingrained reason for you to react to certain situations with negativity. The situation is bringing up a past pain or hurt and your survival instincts are kicking in to tell you that there is a problem and that you need to protect yourself. As you wait and breathe into the moment, you will become more aligned with reality and more conscious. You can then speak from the power of the present moment rather than the pain of your past experience. Everyone in your life will appreciate the change and they may even model after you.

It is also helpful to remember that you do not have to be perfect. Some days, you may be tired or stressed and you might slip into old patterns. If you react too quickly and notice that you do, simply apologize to the person you reacted to. People respond compassionately when you take ownership for your actions and apologize. The person may even gain respect for you because of your self-awareness. It is incredibly healing to admit your mistakes. The sooner you do, the sooner you can let them go.

Respond Rather Than React Overview

Key Practice Steps:

1. When you feel upset, pause before you speak. Respond rather than react.

2. Learn to recognize the difference between an unconscious emotional reaction and your inner wisdom.

3. Apologize if you overreact, forgive yourself immediately and let it go.

Your Personal Goal: _____

_____

_____

_____

_____

_____

_____

"Before you speak, ask yourself: Is it kind, is it true, is it necessary, does it improve upon the silence?"

-Shirdi Sai Baba

5

Let Go of Limiting Beliefs

Affirmation:
"I can do anything I set my mind to."

The mind has the ability to create a positive, beautiful life, but it also has the ability to hold us back from our true potential. Simply believing you cannot do something inhibits your action. To be your strongest, most empowered self, it is necessary to notice patterns of limitation. Phrases like, "I can't do that," or, "I am not good enough for this," will slow you down or even prevent you from overcoming obstacles. Once you learn to believe in yourself and your potential, you will be significantly closer to accomplishing your goals.

As a sensitive soul, you may have felt deep hurt in the past when someone has told you that you were not good at something or when you did not accomplish what you set out to do. This may have held you back from discovering your true potential. However, the only way to grow is to move forward, even when you are not perfect at something, and continue to push yourself (even a little bit) out of your comfort zone.

Letting go of limiting beliefs does not mean that stepping out of your comfort zone and believing in yourself will be easy or that you will feel 100% confident in everything you do. It means that you can feel the fear of the unknown and move forward anyway, believing that while you may not know everything now, you have the strength and determination to learn as you go. As you repeat positive words toward yourself about your abilities, you simultaneously let go of the fear that keeps you stuck in your tracks. It is okay to make mistakes and to try something twenty times before you get it right. In fact, this is truly the only way to succeed.

Every successful person has made countless mistakes, but they used their mistakes as lessons and motivation to continue forward on the path to their dreams. They didn't give up at the first "no." The fear of failure is generally far worse than actually failing because through your action, you will learn valuable lessons to take with you for the future. Know that sometimes you need to feel fear to grow.

When I spend time with babies and young children, I am reminded that every single thing I know today, I did not know at one time. It reminds me to have confidence that I can always learn something new. I remember after graduating as a wellness coach, I was afraid to start seeing clients. I thought I was too young, too inexperienced, and too shy. One day, a yoga student of mine asked me if I could coach her and I said yes before I had time to worry about it. I was exceptionally nervous for that first meeting, but it only took that one session for me to realize that I could most definitely be a wellness coach. The same thing happened for me with teaching yoga, doing wellness talks, and even becoming an author. You have to take that first step to find out what you are capable of.

Where in your life are you limiting yourself? What do you think you are not capable of (but really are)? What excuses are you making for yourself to not live up to your potential? Make a list of a few areas in which you think you are holding yourself back. Visualize yourself succeeding in those areas. Then, create specific affirmations to turn those thoughts around. For example, if you think, "I am such a bad cook," start cooking and telling yourself, "My cooking skills are constantly improving." There is no such thing as being bad at something, only lack of practice and a discouraged mindset. You can do anything you set your mind to.

Let Go of Limiting Beliefs Overview

Key Practice Steps:

1. Avoid setting limits on your potential or under-estimating what you are capable of.

2. Speak only positive words about your skills and abilities. Avoid saying you can't do something or are not good enough.

3. Allow yourself to feel some fear and move forward anyway.

Where in your life are you holding yourself back?

- _____

- _____

- _____

Your Personal Goal: _____

_____

_____

_____

"Whether you think you can or
think you can't, you're right."

-Henry Ford

6

Visualization

Affirmation:
*"I use my mind to envision and
create positive outcomes."*

Visualization is an incredibly effective way to empower your mind to create the reality you want in the future while simultaneously bringing more peace and joy into your life in the present moment. Visualization is the act of imagining in your "mind's eye" the exact conditions that you want for your future in as much detail as possible. The aim is to experience your visualization as if you are already there. To get the best results, be as detail oriented and specific as possible; truly see yourself in the picture. What do you feel like? What does it look like? Who is with you? What do you smell, taste, hear, feel, or see? Focus on the best possible conditions with the most attention to how those conditions make you feel. After all, while we have many goals and aspirations in our lives, the real purpose of those goals is always to feel a certain way. Maybe you want to feel joy, peace, or pride. Maybe you want to feel strong, confident, happy, or relaxed. Maybe you want to feel all of those things! Go ahead and try as best as you can to feel those things as you visualize. This is your life to live and it is your birthright to pursue your dreams. For your dreams to come true, you have to believe in them.

Even if you are skeptical about this, give it a try and experience the power of visualization for yourself. Visualization is not a replacement for real life of course, and it doesn't mean your dreams will magically come true, but when combined with consistent action on your part, it is a powerful tool to help you move towards those dreams with confidence and clarity. At its most basic level, it helps you figure out what your dreams are so that you can more effectively chase after them and be more aware of it when you do achieve them. Only when you truly know what you want, and you know it so well that you can **visualize** the outcome, can you actually get there. How could you possibly get where you want to go if you don't know where "there" is? This doesn't mean that you need to know everything about how you want the rest of your life to go. It just means that day-by-day, with practice, you can begin to picture more and more of the future you want to create for yourself.

Not only can you use visualization to imagine the future of your dreams, but you can use it to imagine any upcoming situation, such as a big interview or an important life occasion going as well as possible. Our thoughts are the energy that drive our actions. Your focus creates a self-fulfilling prophecy. If you are thinking and focusing about what could go wrong, you are actually embracing opportunities for more things to go wrong. As sensitive souls, worry often overwhelms us and we spend our time inadvertently visualizing what we don't want to happen. We may have a tendency to look at things in worst case scenarios. Avoid thinking thoughts like, "I just know this interview isn't going to go well." Instead, use your imagination and words to think of everything that could go right. Instead say, "I can see myself shining in the interview and getting the job." See in your mind your best possible scenario.

As a sensitive soul with a creative imagination,

you don't need much time devoted to visualization for it to have a powerful impact. Even just a few minutes a day can be enough. The more attention you pay to how these visualizations make you feel, the better you will feel in the moment and the more positivity and tangibility you will associate with your dreams. I love to visualize right before I go to sleep. I am already lying down and comfortable and I have a little time to think of the best things that could happen while I slowly drift off into sleep. I always feel so happy and relaxed when I picture my future.

Maybe you have a different time of day that you like to visualize. See what works for you. I recommend being in a comfortable place with your eyes closed so that you can fully relax and are not distracted by what you see or other things going on around you. As a sensitive soul, you will likely be quite positively impacted by images in your mind, and my guess is that you will thoroughly enjoy doing this and want to continue indefinitely.

Another practice to help visualize the future that I recommend (and personally enjoy) is creating a vision board. You simply find pictures, words, phrases, or quotes that you love and want to represent your future, paste them onto a board in a way that resonates with you, and then admire the board daily. You might consider taking a picture of the board on your phone so that it is always with you to look at. You can make a few separate boards for different areas of your life or make one for your life as a whole. Since your dreams and goals are always updating, periodically create new vision boards to continue that process of growth.

Keep in mind that visualization does not mean simply

thinking about what you want then sitting back and waiting for the universe to provide you with all you ask for. You must continue to take steps forward in the direction of your dreams. Opportunities cannot come to you when you are not doing your best to move forward with your plans. You must act. It is also important to note that you do not need to know how you are going to get where you want to go. Our paths are always unknown, so your job is only to visualize and continue to take steps forward, giving your best to the task at hand. One thing will lead to another, but doing nothing will not lead to anything. Don't second guess yourself, continue to act in the direction of your dreams in the best way you know how. This does not mean that you should overwork yourself in the process of moving toward your dreams. As you know, self-care is always going to be essential to your sensitive soul so you don't burn out or overwhelm yourself. Take it one small step at a time.

It is helpful to also make sure that you are not spending too much time visualizing and not enough time being present in your life. Allow the visualization to inspire you and help you feel joy, but not to make you feel that where you are now isn't good enough. You are always exactly where you need to be. Allow yourself to be present in the moment as much as you can. If you are spending too much time visualizing, you will not be able to act, and in turn, you will lessen the chances of getting where you want to go, leaving you unhappy with the present moment. When you use visualization intentionally, you can stay present in your visualization, feel the feelings you want for your life, and simultaneously work toward your beautiful future.

Visualization Overview

Key Practice Steps:

1. Practice visualization daily. Visualize as much detail as possible and practice feeling the joy you will feel when you are in that future situation.
2. When you find yourself visualizing something negative or overemphasizing worry, close your eyes and instead visualize all the good that can happen.
3. Act in the direction of your dreams and visualizations even if you don't know exactly how to get there.

Your Personal Goal: _____

_____

_____

_____

_____

_____

_____

"The secret of change is to focus all of your energy not on fighting the old, but on building the new."

-Socrates

7

Be Present

Affirmation:

"I am at peace in the present moment."

Do you have trouble enjoying the moment? Many of us are so ruled by our fear of the future and regret over the past, combined with an inability to be still, that we are rarely present in the now. Our culture is so focused on multitasking and being busy that many people actually feel bad about themselves when they are not doing more than one thing at a time or doing something "productive." Unfortunately, multitasking leads to an inability to enjoy the moment.

Being present means doing whatever you are doing (one thing) with your full attention. The present moment is all we ever have, so if you cannot enjoy the moment, essentially, you cannot enjoy your life. As a sensitive soul, you may feel called to be like everyone else and try to do multiple tasks at once, but you likely know deep down that this way of being rarely serves you. You feel best when you take your time and focus on whatever is happening in the present moment.

Just like anything, learning to be more present takes practice. Pay attention to your body, your tasks, and your thoughts. You'll notice your thoughts becoming distracted but then you'll bring them back to the task at hand. Your body is always present. It always shows up for the moment, so we can learn to bring the mind into the present moment by focusing on the body. Bring your attention to where you feel sensation in the body. Feel what it is like to be alive in this moment. Feel the movement of the breath in the torso and in the nostrils. Feel your whole body simultaneously, and then continue your task/activity with this subtle awareness of your body.

Recently, one of my clients complained that if she was present all the time then how could she prepare for the future? Would everything fall apart? It seems impossible! These are only excuses to not learn how to be present. Being present does not mean only just thinking about the present, rather it means focusing on the present task, your present state of mind, and your present feelings. If you set aside time to plan for the future and focus on that planning specifically, then you are planning in a present state of mind. If fact, planning is a vital aspect of being able to be fully present. Once you have made your plan, you know what you are doing in the moment is exactly what you are want to be doing so you can give it the full attention it deserves and be less likely to be distracted by other tasks. Once you learn to be more present, you will recognize that anxiety about the future will not empower you because the future is always unknown. You can never handle the unknown, but you can always handle the now.

Like many people, I often struggle with being present, especially when working on the computer. There are so many distractions. To help combat this, I will close my email and social media and set a timer for a specific task. For example, currently my timer is set to work on my book for one hour. I have made a commitment to myself to not do anything except work on my book until the timer sounds. Once the timer sounds, I will either choose to continue for another set amount of time or set a timer to work on a different task. I like to pick the amount of time based on my energy for the day, but there has been discussion about the high effectiveness of doing tasks in twenty-five minute intervals, so this could be a good place to start. I am always amazed at how much more relaxed and accomplished I feel when I stick to one thing at a time.

One of the best ways to stay present, enjoy what you do, and feel satisfied when a task is complete is simply to take your time and do it well. So many of us rush through our tasks. This way of behaving generally does not leave a lot of room to be satisfied with your work. Take even one minute to plan out how you will do something, stay focused and relaxed during the task, and then admire the end result. When done with care, most any task can be fulfilling—even tasks that you may normally dislike such as doing the dishes or going grocery shopping. Even if you are able to rush through a task and do it fairly well, it is likely that you will not feel satisfied because you will have created a stress response in your body from rushing. You may end up feeling on edge and begin thinking right away about what else needs to get done rather than feeling any gratification in what you accomplished. Before I begin a task, I will often set an intention to work at a relaxed pace and enjoy the task for what it is. Sometimes I forget halfway through, but then I notice I was rushing and I have the opportunity to become present again.

I always recommend experimenting to find out what is right for you, as we learn best through investigation and self-study. Next time you have a task that you would normally do without much thought, take your time to do your best and see what happens. Notice how you feel while you are preforming the task and then notice the sense of satisfaction that comes from completion. You will feel more content with your life as a whole when you learn to find gratification in the little moments.

Where in your life do you need to be more present? Consider making a list so that you can bring more awareness to these activities. When you find yourself distracted, try focusing on your breath to help you come back to the present moment. You can practice coming back to the breath when you find your mind drifting off in a conversation, while washing the dishes, or driving your car. In many situations, it is highly effective to use your breath to help you regain focus. Try it right now. Focus your attention on the feelings in your body and the movement of the breath in your belly. Feel your belly rise on the inhalation and fall on the exhalation. Recognize that **the present moment holds all the power you will ever need**. Practice coming home to your body and you will learn to connect with the stillness and peace that is already within you.

Be Present Overview

Key Practice Steps:

1. Make a list of where you need to be more present in your life and then practice being more present in those areas.
2. Limit multitasking and rushing. Learn to take satisfaction in the smallest of tasks.
3. Focus your attention back on your breath and body when you lose presence.

Where in your life do you need to be more present?

- _____

- _____

- _____

Your Personal Goal: _____

_____

_____

_____

"The point of power is always
in the present moment."

-Louise Hay

8

Open Your Mind

Affirmation:
*"I am open to new possibilities
and new ways of thinking."*

The older we get, the more we tend to get stuck in old patterns of belief and to identify with them as truths rather than seeing them as simply beliefs. We often get intensely attached to right or wrong and forget to explore the opposite perspective to see what we can take away from it. In order to grow and evolve in this life, we need to be open-minded. We need to be open to new experiences, new ideas, and new ways of being. We need to go beyond our emotional reactions and look at life from a broad range of perspectives.

Not being open-minded cuts you off from experiencing life fully. Do you ever find yourself not even listening to what someone has to say because you have already decided that they are wrong? Instead of listening intently with an open mind, are you thinking of all the reasons why you disagree? Next time you are in this situation, take a deep breath, be present, and really listen to the person rather than the mental chatter in your mind.

You can train yourself to be more understanding and open to other people's perspectives. Look for what is right about someone's point of view rather than looking only for fault. Ask for details as to why someone feels the way they do. You may not end up agreeing with what the person has said, but you will at least have a better understanding of where they are coming from and how that person experiences the world.

Read articles or watch videos from a different perspective than your own. Don't discount something immediately because it is new to you; stay curious and allow yourself the opportunity to evolve your own understanding. It is true that the more you know, the more you know you don't know, so embrace all there is to learn. Our collective knowledge is constantly increasing. Not being open-minded will keep you stuck in the past and disconnected from your true potential.

As a sensitive soul, you may find that it is too hard in the moment to think of a conflicting perspective and may benefit from taking time later that day to think about it on your own. I find that writing helps me see something from the other person's perspective more clearly. You will likely be pleased to see how your negative emotions will soften when you can at least somewhat understand where they are coming from. Right and wrong then become less defined. When you become adept at broadening your perspective, you become much more intelligent and empowered. It is always impressive to see someone gracefully change his or her opinion when presented with compelling evidence. Being able to listen to someone with an open mind and without judgment will bring you great respect and will further your growth as a human being.

Open Your Mind Overview

Key Practice Steps:

1. Open yourself to new ideas and different ways of thinking.

2. Listen to other perspectives without judgment.

3. Be open-minded enough to change your opinion when presented with compelling evidence.

Your Personal Goal: _____

_____

_____

_____

_____

_____

_____

"An open mind allows you to explore and create and grow. Remember that progress would be impossible if we always did things the way we always have."

-Dr. Wayne Dyer

9

Organization

Affirmation:
*"I keep my life and possessions
neat and organized."*

I see many clients who are overwhelmed by clutter and being held back mentally by the accumulation of personal belongings. Is this something you struggle with? The difficulty with organization may come from buying too many things, not having a designated space for your things, having trouble letting go of things you no longer need, or simply not putting your items away properly. The more items you have, the harder the challenge. As a sensitive soul, you may not have a problem with clutter in the traditional sense, but even not being as tidy as you would like to be can cause you to feel unsettled. An organized space signifies an organized mind and an organized life. By simply organizing your outer world, your inner world will make a dramatic shift.

Sensitive souls are generally drawn to peace, beauty, and a feeling of ease in their space. Clutter and disorganization create a lack of ease and potentially an inability to relax fully. You want to create a home that feels like a sanctuary, a safe place in the world to rest, not a place that creates unnecessary disorder. Your home is a representation of you, so you want to treat your home and possessions as you would ideally treat yourself—with love and respect.

One of my favorite books about organization is by Marie Kondo, aptly called, *The Life Changing Magic of Tidying Up*. In her book, she encourages readers to get rid of anything that does not "spark joy." I found this technique extremely effective and recommend that you consider doing it too. As you go through your belongings, you will likely find that, intuitively, you know what to keep and what to get rid of based on the joy you feel (or do not feel) when you hold that item. Do you love it? Do you need it? If the answers are no, you can let it go. If you cannot let go of old things, you are subconsciously choosing to value your past over your future.

As you learn to let go of old possessions, you will likely find you are less interested in buying more things and more meticulous with what you do buy. While buying something new can be exciting, soon after the purchase, it is highly likely that you lose enthusiasm about that item and want something new. Once you have de-cluttered and organized, you will value the feeling of space and ease in your home over the short-lived rush of shopping. Having a more thoughtful, simple approach to your home also means that it will be easier to keep your space tidy. Imagine the feeling of living in an organized space, surrounded only by items that you love. Does it feel like a sigh of relief?

If reading about getting rid of clutter gives you a rush of positive emotion, I recommend getting started right away. Powerful changes in your life can happen when you learn to let go of what is no longer needed in your home. These changes can then permeate into your work, relationships, family, and practically every aspect of your life.

I have a client who is a serial entrepreneur. He is talented and bright and values organization highly, but was bogged down with doing too many projects at once. During one session, he mentioned that his workspace was quite disorganized, which I found significant considering his interest in organization. He said that he liked the feeling of having all of his things close to him and rarely ever got rid of anything old. As a simple step toward a more organized and present workday, I recommended he de-clutter his workspace before doing anything else. I guided him to let go of his need to be surrounded by so many things at once, and instead, to have only items that he truly loved or needed. To my excitement, the week after he completed his clutter busting, he informed me that he changed his plans and was now going to focus only on the one big project he saw the most potential in. By getting rid of his excess stuff, he was finally able to think more clearly and regain focus. Try this for yourself and see what happens. It may take a lot of work, but it will be well worth it.

Organization Overview

Key Practice Steps:

1. Go through your possessions and let go of anything that does not spark joy.

2. Keep your space neat and organized.

3. Treat your possessions with love and respect.

Your Personal Goal: _____

_____

_____

_____

_____

_____

_____

"Declutter the mess in your home and heart.
Don't let your past crowd out your future."

- Dr. Thema Bryant-Davis

10

Limit Electronics

Affirmation:
"I take time away from technology
so that I can connect to myself."

We have amazing works of technology right at our fingertips all day long. We are connected to people all over the world and we have the ability to learn more than we could ever imagine with the click of a mouse. You may feel the appeal to be constantly connected to cyberspace for all of its immense value, but in the meantime, you lose your connection with yourself.

As a sensitive soul, you may likely find that you are sensitive to the energy of electronic devices. You may feel overstimulated, and consequently, agitated from using them or being around them too consistently. It has become so common to use electronics all of the time that you may not even realize that this may be part of why you feel so overstimulated or why you cannot relax easily.

Technology can be addictive. For example, every time we get a new follower or a new "like" the reward center in our brain lights up, which makes us feel good. Unfortunately, this good feeling is short lived, leaving us wanting more. I have a client who was spending hours of her time in the evening after work on social media. She admitted that she always ended up feeling discouraged and frustrated with herself when she was done, but she couldn't get herself to stop. I recommended she give herself twenty-five minutes of guilt-free social media, and when the timer sounded, she had to log off immediately. This ended up being the perfect solution for her because she logged on, prepared to do what she needed to do, wrote back to any messages she had, and made the most of her time. She then logged off feeling satisfied but not overstimulated. Is there something similar that you feel addicted or drawn to in a way you feel is not in your best interest?

What is the first thing you do in the morning? If you check your email, I highly recommend you take some time to do something for yourself first. Take a shower, meditate, practice your affirmations and start your day off on a positive note rather than diving into work or your to-do list. If you check your email first, you start your day off in reaction to what you see rather than with your own intention. This can negatively affect the progress of your whole day.

It is a great idea to also stop using electronic devices one hour before bedtime. The light from your devices keeps you stimulated and awake and your body needs time to transition into sleep without that high stimulation. I also highly recommend taking periodic electronic vacations. Consider committing to one day a month without any electronics. Once you experience a relaxing day with no electronics, you will want to do it again and again. It is important to set a specific goal for yourself around your technology usage, otherwise it will be hard to make any progress.

This topic is especially meaningful for the younger generations. You may see everyone else on their phone 24/7 and feel like that is a completely normal thing for a human to do, but this is the first time in history we have had this amazing technology, and there has not been enough time to truly understand the potential negative mental and physical effects of being connected to technology so continuously. You can still go on frequently, but make sure you take long breaks and that you are being mindful with your time.

Limit Electronics Overview

Key Practice Steps:

1. Avoid checking your email first thing in the morning.

2. Stop using electronics at least one hour before bedtime. Start small and work your way up.

3. Take periodic electronic vacations and set specific goals around usage.

Your Personal Goal: _____

_____

_____

_____

_____

_____

_____

"The human spirit must prevail over technology."

-Albert Einstein

11

Let Go of the Little Things

Affirmation:
*"I easily let go of little troubles.
I know what truly matters."*

Do you have a tendency to "sweat the small stuff?" Do you spend time fussing about things that, in the big picture, are rather trivial? Do you get frustrated because you spilled your tea, because you forgot to call the dentist before 5pm, or because your co-worker ate your last banana? While a bit frustrating, none of those kinds of things are worth holding onto any negative emotion about. You will soon forget that any of these things ever happened, so the sooner you let them go, the better off you will be. Being bothered by minor things will do nothing to benefit you and will majorly reduce your sense of wellbeing. By starting with the intention that you can easily let go of the little troubles, you begin to create space in your life to pause, think about a situation, and then respond more calmly.

I notice that a lot of people allow themselves to become upset by little things, and as a sensitive being, you are even more likely to be sensitive to disruptions in your day or other occurrences that do not go as you wished they would. Next time you get upset, take a moment to access how important what you are upset about is. Take a deep breath, and then ask yourself what the benefit of being upset is and how you would feel if you let go of your frustration. For the little things, the answer to these questions will always be that there is no benefit to being upset and you would feel much better to let it go. Then you have the power to decide if you want to be upset with no benefit or if you want to free yourself from pain by choosing to consciously let it go. The answer is simple. Choose not to create unnecessary pain for yourself.

At first, it may feel challenging, but it takes simply being able to successfully let something go a few times before it becomes a routine. Notice the feeling of liberation that comes from taking control over the situation and not letting your emotions dictate how you respond. You may even feel a rush of positive energy from knowing that you responded to the situation in a strong and empowered manner. Each time you take control in this way, the respect you have for yourself will grow.

Where in your life do you tend to get upset about the little things? For me, one of my biggest areas was driving, especially in my home city of Boston. I would be having a nice day, and then get into my car and immediately feel tense and anxious due to poor road conditions and frantic drivers. I dreaded being in the car, which was unfortunate because my work at the time revolved around driving in traffic to multiple locations each day. Once I brought more awareness to the situation and recognized what small matters these were, I began to look at driving as a way to practice kindness and patience. Instead of being annoyed that someone was trying to cut in front of me, I let the car in. I chose to smile instead of honk. I am not always a perfect driver, but I feel so much better about driving and about myself on the road than I did before.

Look at the areas in your life that you know you get

easily annoyed with and see them as opportunities to grow. I recommend making a list of things you worry about unnecessarily so you can keep them in mind for future situations. When those situations arise, you can remember your list and practice more easily letting the feeling of frustration go. Make sure to be kind to yourself as you practice. Being upset that you got upset will also be of no benefit to you. Continue to practice taking control of your mental attitude while loving and accepting yourself every step of the way.

Let Go of the Little Things Overview

Key Practice Steps:

1. Bring awareness to the things you stress over unnecessarily and practice taking control of those feelings by consciously choosing to let them go when they arise.

2. When upset, take a deep breath, and ask yourself if this truly matters. If the answer is no, let it go.

3. Be kind to yourself if you get upset about something unimportant. The fact that you brought awareness to that feeling is a win in and of itself.

What do you tend to stress about unnecessarily?

- _____

- _____

- _____

Your Personal Goal: _____

_____

_____

"Ask yourself the question,
will this matter a year from now?"

-Richard Carlson

12

Release Perfectionism

Affirmation:
*"My best is always good enough.
I release the need to be perfect."*

As a sensitive soul, you are likely to struggle with perfectionist tendencies. You may have even felt overwhelmed while reading this book so far and had the thought, "Oh no, I have so many improvements to make, I am not good enough," instead of feeling excited for the potential for growth. I want you to use this opportunity to let go of perfectionism and to allow yourself to be complete and whole exactly as you are while also accepting room for growth. Life is long. To live an empowered life, it is imperative to always be learning and growing. Learn from the obstacles in front of you and improve your resiliency. No one does everything with perfection; the nature of being human is imperfection. Willingness to both accept imperfection and adopt change are key to living a balanced and empowered life.

As a kid (like me), you may have thought that adults knew everything and that once you grew up you would know everything too. Perhaps you even thought that at eighteen or twenty-one you would magically become an "adult." However, once you reached the age that you thought you would become an adult, you likely found that, to your surprise, you still didn't know everything yet! In fact, life continued to appear more complex than you had originally anticipated and you realized that what I mentioned before holds true—the more you know, the more you know you don't know. This may have fostered a strong sense of anxiety, never feeling like you are enough because you are still holding onto that idea from childhood that you will be able to get to a point where you know everything (like everyone else). If this resonates with you, send yourself some love and know that no one, absolutely no one, knows everything. No one is perfect. Allow me to reiterate. No one is perfect and you are no exception. Are you relieved?

You may have mistakenly been living with the idea that perfectionism is a noble quality. This is simply untrue. Perfectionism is a shield; it is something that is used to keep you stuck, to not allow progress, and to give you excuses as to why you can't do something. At the root of perfectionism is always fear. More specifically, it is the fear of not being good enough. As you learn to love and accept yourself, you'll find that you are already good enough for yourself, and that you always were. Most importantly, you must allow yourself to embrace your fear and put yourself out there so that you can manifest the opportunity to grow. Otherwise, you risk creating a very real self-fulfilling prophecy of limiting your own growth by believing you are not good enough to try.

In most situations, someone will praise you and someone else will criticize or question you regardless of the action you take. There are too many independent mentalities in the world to realistically please everyone; it is impossible and an enormous waste of energy. Perfectionism holds you back from making mistakes and taking chances, and it is those mistakes and chances that will bring you the most experience and wisdom. Know that the search for self-improvement is never ending, and while you may want to improve in some ways, you are simultaneously whole and complete just as you are. Stand up today and say, "I am whole just as I am. I release the need to be perfect."

Take some time to think about the specific areas of your life that you feel you have the most perfectionist tendencies. Is it in your relationships? Your profession? Being a parent? How can you honor all that you do with love and allow for room for improvement at the same time? You have likely been struggling with perfectionism for a long time, so accept that it may be a slow process of noticing when you are being too hard on yourself and taking small steps toward releasing perfectionist tendencies.

As you reflect on the topics we have covered in the next section, be kind to yourself. Give yourself permission to not be perfect. See opportunities for growth as exciting rather than necessary for you to be worthy. Take it one step at a time. It has taken me about fifteen years of active searching and practice to make these topics part of my core self, and many days, I forget and have to remind myself again. That is okay. Embrace your journey. We all have more to learn.

Release Perfectionism Overview

Key Practice Steps:

1. Recognize that, at its core, perfectionism is fear that you are not good enough.
2. Bring awareness to the specific places in your life where you tend to be the hardest on yourself.
3. Accept and care for yourself without needing to be perfect. Allow yourself to let go of perfectionism.

Where do you limit yourself with perfectionism?

- _____
- _____
- _____

Your Personal Goal: _____

_____

_____

_____

"Perfectionism is a twenty-ton shield that
we lug around thinking it will protect us when,
in fact, it's the thing that's really preventing
us from being seen and taking flight."

-Brené Brown

PART 4

Your Transformation

Affirmation:
"I am willing to change."

We often know what we need to do to change, but have trouble getting the results we are hoping for. The most powerful piece of advice I can offer to help you truly transform your life is to make a sincere commitment to your goals, even if you do not know exactly how to accomplish them yet. Thinking you need to know the path before you commit will keep you stuck in your tracks or cause you to give up when you come to a crossroads. The only way to transform is to experiment, explore and continue moving forward, trusting yourself as you go. While there may be many twists and turns along the way, with a sincere commitment, you will eventually get where you want to go.

Don't wait for the perfect time to start or for someone to tell you the magic fix you may be looking for. Know that you hold the power of transformation within you just as you are now. Although they may help significantly, no one doctor, healer, teacher, mentor, or therapist can do it for you. You have the opportunity in every moment to take control over your life and to move in a positive and empowering direction. You just have to fully commit yourself to the opportunity.

It is essential to keep in mind that many changes take significant time and patience to integrate. This is actually beneficial because a change that you have slowly worked toward will be much more sustainable. If you are expecting a quick fix, you will likely become disheartened and give up because you aren't making progress fast enough. Alternatively, the quick fix may end up backfiring, leaving you right back where you started (or worse). Refuse to hold yourself back from your true potential by not committing to your goals just because you cannot see the exact path ahead of you. Stay the course. If you know the exact steps of your path ahead of time, it is likely not your path. Your path will always have elements of mystery and unpredictability. That is just the way life works.

Another important key to transformation is a willingness to change. Perhaps there are many sections of the book that you are very willing and excited to change, such as adding a daily gratitude practice or committing to a more regular yoga schedule. While this is excellent, you might not be getting to the heart of what will really transform your life in a big way. For powerful transformation, it is important to also focus on the areas that you are feeling uneasy about changing or ones that may have even triggered your sensitive soul. Do you hate the idea of accepting what is? This may be because it is exactly what you need to do.

If you are not truly open and willing to change anything that comes up for you, you will continuously hit a wall until you allow yourself to go deeper into the transformation you truly need. It does not have to be today, but eventually, you'll need to go right into the heart of what ails your sensitive soul and then learn to love that part of you into change. Not being open to change will close you off from the true healing powers of the universe.

The beginning of this next section will teach you about the stages of change in relation to this book and help you figure out which areas you need to work on most. After that, there are exercises to help you go deeper into setting your goals, committing to them, and envisioning your future. Please don't skip the exercises. If you cannot do them now, I recommend scheduling a time when you can commit to doing them. The exercises will take approximately twenty-five minutes. They will help you clarify what you need to work on as well as give you a plan to move forward with confidence. It can also be very fun and enlightening to look back on these exercises in the future and notice how much you have grown.

"Once a person is determined to help themselves, there is nothing that can stop them."

-Nelson Mandela

The Four Stages of Transformation

To help understand where you are on your path of transformation for each topic, you may find it helpful to follow these four stages: Pain Point, Awareness, Practice, and Integration. Use these stages as guides to help you move forward with your goals. Remember, even recognizing that something is a problem is a critical first step.

Stage 1: Pain Point – You notice something in your life is causing you pain. You recognize that you do not want this pain anymore, but are not necessarily aware of what is causing it or how to change it. You start to investigate what could be causing the pain.

Example: Emily regularly feels tired and bloated after she eats. This distresses her, but she has not yet thought about the cause. She starts to pay more attention to her food.

Stage 2: Awareness – You become aware of something you need to work on relating to your pain. You may have known this deep down for a while but could not admit it to yourself. Now you know for sure. You feel the direct connection between your pain and this issue. This is an exciting step because you are now much closer to true transformation as you know what you need to do.

Example: Through becoming more aware of her eating, Emily recognizes that her fatigue and bloating set in when she has eaten too much too fast. She now knows what she needs to do.

Stage 3: Committed Practice – You commit to making a change, even if you do not know exactly how to change yet. You will likely revert back to old patterns many times, but you keep working toward your goal. You are gentle with yourself along the way, not punishing yourself with change, but changing because you love yourself.

Example: Emily commits to slowing down her eating. She tries to remember during her meals, but frequently forgets. She does her best to be kind to herself if she has eaten too fast and to learn from her mistakes. She tries various techniques to help her slow down like repeating an intention before her meal, chewing each bite thirty times, using chopsticks, and putting her utensil down between bites.

Stage 4: Integration – You get to a point where this change no longer takes a lot of effort. You have seen the benefits and you do not want go back. You may sometimes forget and slip back into old patterns, but deep down, the inner shift has been made and it will not be forgotten. Welcome to the new you.

Example: Emily has practiced daily and has trained herself to be a slow eater about 90% of the time. Her fatigue, bloating, and overeating have greatly reduced due to her new pace. She feels proud of herself and has no desire to go back to being a fast eater.

Keep in Mind: Transformation will always be an ongoing process because life is an ongoing process. It is okay and expected to forget sometimes and to go back to your old habits. The most important thing is to continue forward, not give up and love yourself along the way.

Where Are You Ready to Grow?

The following pages offer a survey to help you determine which areas are most significant for you to work on at this time. The survey is also available on my website so you can take it multiple times to track your progress. For each of the items, rate yourself on a scale of 1-5. Please rate yourself a 1 if you feel you need drastic improvement and a 5 if you feel totally satisfied in that area. Answer the questions with your first instinct and be as honest with yourself as you can. If you are truly not sure how to answer a certain item, ask a close friend or family member for their input on where they think you have room for improvement. Please check back to the correlating sections in the book if you need clarification before you rate yourself.

Scale of 1-5

1. This is incredibly challenging for me. I need all the help I can get.

2. I need to do significant work in this area.

3. I need to do work in this area.

4. I feel good overall but could benefit from some fine-tuning.

5. I feel comfortable and confident in this area.

Part 1: Body

1.	Healing Whole Foods	1	2	3	4	5
2.	Relaxed Eating	1	2	3	4	5
3.	Hydration	1	2	3	4	5
4.	Posture	1	2	3	4	5
5.	Joyful Movement	1	2	3	4	5
6.	Slowing Down	1	2	3	4	5
7.	Breathing	1	2	3	4	5
8.	Relaxation	1	2	3	4	5
9.	Nature	1	2	3	4	5
10.	Sleep	1	2	3	4	5
11.	Cut Back on Chemicals	1	2	3	4	5
12.	Continue to Explore	1	2	3	4	5

Part 2: Heart

1.	Self-Love	1	2	3	4	5
2.	Compassion	1	2	3	4	5
3.	Trust Yourself	1	2	3	4	5
4.	Express Your Feelings	1	2	3	4	5
5.	Prioritize Yourself	1	2	3	4	5
6.	Appreciation	1	2	3	4	5
7.	Accept Constructive Criticism	1	2	3	4	5
8.	Forgiveness	1	2	3	4	5
9.	Eliminate Negative Comparisons	1	2	3	4	5
10.	Protect Your Energy	1	2	3	4	5

11. Choose Love	1	2	3	4	5
12. Ways to Find Balance	1	2	3	4	5

Part 3: Mind

1. Choose a Positive Outlook	1	2	3	4	5
2. Accept What Is	1	2	3	4	5
3. Choose Your Words Thoughtfully	1	2	3	4	5
4. Respond Rather Than React	1	2	3	4	5
5. Let Go of Limiting Beliefs	1	2	3	4	5
6. Visualization	1	2	3	4	5
7. Be Present	1	2	3	4	5
8. Open Your Mind	1	2	3	4	5
9. Organization	1	2	3	4	5
10. Limit Electronics	1	2	3	4	5
11. Let Go of the Little Things	1	2	3	4	5
12. Release Perfectionism	1	2	3	4	5

Goals

Review your survey and look for your three lowest rated categories. Consider these your main opportunities for growth. If there are ties, choose the three that stand out to you the most or the ones you feel most ready to tackle. From those three, take a moment to write a few sentences about the aspects of that area that are most challenging for you and what your goal or intention is for that area moving forward. Include the stage of change you are at, if applicable. Use this information to determine what to put your attention on first.

If possible, make sure that your goals are specific, reasonable, and time bound.

Example

Opportunity for growth: My house is disorganized and I can never find what I need when I need it. I feel overwhelmed by my clutter and can't relax. I can't live this way anymore.

Weak Goal: I will become organized.

Strong Goal: I will organize my house one room at a time, getting rid of all the possessions that do not bring me joy. I will allow myself two weeks to work on each room and will complete the project in three months.

Opportunity for growth #1 _____

_____

_____

Goal: _____

_____

_____

_____

Opportunity for growth #2 _____

_____

_____

Goal: _____

_____

_____

_____

Opportunity for growth #3 _____

_____

_____

Goal: _____

_____

_____

_____

Moving Forward

For the next month (or whatever is best for your schedule), commit to working toward these goals. After the month is over, re-evaluate, either casually or by retaking the survey. From there, you can decide if you need to continue to work on those goals or if you are ready to move on to new ones. Remember, it is important to take your time and not overwhelm yourself. More is not always better. If working on three goals at once feels like way too much, slow down and do one or two at a time. You can always come back to them later.

Commitment Affirmations

It is important to have affirmations that you can use to reinforce your goals. Let's create commitment affirmations for you to begin repeating ten times when you wake up in the morning and ten times when you go to bed at night. The more you use the affirmation, the better, so feel free to repeat it anytime throughout the day, especially if you are feeling discouraged or down. You are welcome to use the affirmations that I provided at the beginning of the sections you are working on or to create your own. Make sure that the affirmations truly resonate with you and that when you speak them, you connect to the words you are saying. Always frame your affirmations in the present tense. You can choose to focus on just the three affirmations that correspond to your goals to start or add as many as you like.

Affirmation Example

Goal: To practice appreciation by journaling about what I am grateful for each morning when I wake up.

Affirmation: I observe and appreciate the blessings in my life, each and every day.

Your Commitment Affirmations:
(Based on your 3 Goals)

1. _____

_____

_____

2. _____

_____

_____

3. _____

_____

_____

Extra Affirmations:

_____

_____

_____

_____

_____

_____

_____

_____

_____

Commitment Letter

Using your most significant goal, write a short letter to yourself committing to this change. Write what pain you are experiencing in this area, what is getting in your way of changing, how you can practice, and how you will feel once this change has been assimilated. How will this change enhance your life? How can you remind yourself to stay on track? Who can help support you in this process? Feel free to use the template below or to write the letter in your own words.

Dear _____,

   I hereby commit to changing _____
_____. This commitment is an act of love toward myself. I am experiencing pain in the form of _____. I no longer want this pain and believe in myself enough to go through the necessary steps to change. Some blockages that are getting in my way of changing are _____
_____. I know I can take control of my situation and practice changing by _____
_____. Once I make this change, I will feel _____.
It will enhance my life in so many ways including
_____.
I will remind myself to stay on track by
_____. The person (or people) that I can recruit to help me is/are _____
_____. I am so excited because I know I can do anything I set my mind to.

With love and admiration,

_____

Visualize Your Future

While focusing on your current goals is an excellent start, it is also helpful to think about the future you want to create for yourself. Use this opportunity to write and envision how you see yourself living in your ideal future. Who do you want to be? How and where do you want to live? Who do you want to spend your time with? How will you take care of yourself? How do you want to feel? What will you achieve personally and professionally? What will your biggest priorities in life be? How do you want to use your gifts to help others? Don't use this as an opportunity to limit yourself, instead dream big. What kind of life do you truly desire?

Write a story about the person you want to become and the life you want to lead in as much detail as you can (the more detail, the better). This story can grow and evolve over time, so make sure you don't get too caught up in the exact details. Choose any timeline that excites you, and if you are not sure, start with ten or twenty years from now. Don't underestimate the power of imagining the future of your dreams. Give this exercise a chance. How can you work toward something you've never imagined?

*I first did this activity ten years ago, and to this day, I still look back on what I wrote and see the correlation with who I am now to what I hoped for in the past. Many of the things I dreamed of have come true (including writing this book!), and sometimes I wonder if they would have if I had not taken the time to think about what I *really* wanted.

My Beautiful Future: _____

_____

_____

_____

_____

_____

_____

_____

_____

_____

_____

_____

_____

_____

_____

_____

_____

_____

_____

_____

_____

_____

_____

_____

Transformation and Beyond

Becoming empowered in body, heart, and mind is a vehicle to finding your true self, living the life of your dreams, and sharing your gifts with the world. It is our calling as human beings to continue to raise our level of consciousness, to take what we have learned from our ancestors and expand on it. If each person were committed to his or her highest goals, we would have peace and community in our world rather than fear and hate. We would work together rather than against each other. You can set an example for those around you by living in alignment with your inner truth and by sharing your empowered yet sensitive soul with the world.

As a sensitive soul, you know by now that you have many special gifts to share such as your compassion, creativity, understanding, intuition, self-awareness, and so much more. Learn to appreciate and be grateful for your sensitive gifts. Share your strengths with those around you. It is easy to feel insignificant, but I promise you, there are so many people who will positively benefit from the gifts you have to offer. Most of the people out in the world, sharing their opinions, are not sensitive souls. The world needs your unique voice, your special perspective, and your sensitive heart. Instead of hiding your gifts, share them!

Remember that we are not meant to go on our life journey alone. To learn and grow, we need someone to support us along the way. We need someone who can hold up a mirror for us, to help us see what we either cannot see or haven't yet been ready to see about ourselves. If you have someone in your life that is willing and able to be that person for you, I recommended discussing your goals with him or her as soon as you can. This may be a best friend, partner, family member, therapist, or coach. Make sure it is someone who understands and appreciates your sensitivity, but who is also willing to help slowly guide you out of your comfort zone. For me, my fiancé was this person. He gently brought things to my attention and modeled for me how to carry myself in the world. I know I had these gifts in me all along, but I don't think that I could have realized it alone. Finding the right person to help you on your journey is invaluable.

Lastly, it is imperative that you make sure to acknowledge your progress along the way. All too frequently, we make a significant change, assimilate it, and then instead of praising ourselves for what we have done, we move right onto our next goal. When this happens, you lose the satisfaction and happiness you were searching for from this change because you did not stop to give yourself credit for it.

It is crucial to acknowledge your progress every step of the way. Profound changes take time and commitment. If you expect them to happen overnight, you will be disappointed. Practice patience with yourself. Take things one-step at a time. If you make a mistake, rather than criticize yourself, send yourself love and compassion. In each and every moment, there is a beautiful opportunity to take a deep breath and start again. Seize that moment.

"May the long time sun shine upon you,
all love surround you, and the pure light
within you, guide your way on."

-old Irish blessing

With Love and Light,

Christie J. Rosen

Appendix A
Overview of Recommended Exercises

PART 1 - BODY

- **10-Days of Clean Eating** – For ten days (or more), eliminate all processed food. If you would like support, visit my website to learn more or to sign up for my next cleanse.

- **Practice Relaxed Eating** – Practice chewing your food well, breathing deeply, and taking time to eat your meal.

- **Posture Check** – Periodically check your posture throughout each day. Hold your body in such a way that you feel strong and well aligned.

- **Practice Joyful Movement** – Make a list of your favorite movement practices and practice one of them often.

- **Notice the Rush** – Make a list of where you tend to rush so you can pay more attention during those activities.

- **Breathing Exercises** – Practice your breathing exercise whenever you can, including practicing long exhalations, three-part breathing, alternate nostril breathing, and/or Lion's Breath.

- **Practice Daily Relaxation** – Find a relaxation practice such as restorative yoga, meditation, guided relaxation, or deep breathing, and practice daily.

- **Create a Morning Routine** – Try to get up at the same time every morning and create a routine that helps you wake up feeling strong and ready for your day.

- **Create an Evening Routine** – Try to go to bed at the same time every night. Take a break from technology before you go to sleep and do something relaxing.

- **Sleep Prioritization** – Write down the benefits you would receive from prioritizing your sleep more highly.

- **Cut Back on Chemicals** – Each time you need a new product, find one that is a healthier, non-toxic choice.

PART 2 - HEART

- **Praise Yourself** – Make a list of what you love about yourself and what you are proud of yourself for. Don't skimp!

- **Practice Compassion** – Practice compassion for those who bother you the most. Try to imagine where they are coming from and recognize the more difficult they are, the more compassion they need.

- **Take Your Own Advice** – For one week, practice not asking for advice and trust your own inner wisdom. Think about what you would tell a friend in the same position.

- **Express Yourself** – Find ways to let your feelings out. Consider consulting a trusted friend, journaling, or seeking professional support.

- **Practice the Quick No and the Slow Yes** – When you don't want to do something, say no right away. When you aren't sure, wait to think about it before you commit.

- **Gratitude Practice** – Choose a gratitude practice to commit to such as writing down ten things you are grateful for each day.

- **Appreciation Practice** – When things aren't going well and you feel upset, ask yourself, "What is there to appreciate in this moment?"

- **Ask for Criticism** – Occasionally ask for constructive criticism from someone you trust to help you become more comfortable with feedback.

- **Practice Forgiveness** – Write a letter from the opposite perspective of your own to help you understand where the person you are in conflict with is coming from. Light a candle, repeat an affirmation, and let it go.

- **Positive Comparison** – When you find yourself jealous of someone, instead note the positive qualities they have and see how you can model after them.

- **Energy Awareness** – Make a list of what drains your energy and what gives you energy.

- **Open Your Heart** - If you feel your heart is closed, sit up tall, place your hands on your heart, breathe deeply, and repeat your heart opening affirmation: "My heart is open. I love freely."

- **Ways to Find Balance** – Make a list of your favorite activities to help you when you feel emotionally out of balance.

PART 3 - MIND

- **Positive Affirmations** – Practice positive affirmations daily. Choose affirmations that resonate with what you need to work on most.

- **Become Aware of Limiting Beliefs** – Make a list of where you limit yourself in your life and be aware when those situations arise. Allow yourself to grow.

- **Visualization** – Spend a few minutes every day envisioning the future of your dreams in as much detail as you can.

- **Become More Present** – Make a list of where you need to be more present in your life and then practice paying more attention in those situations.

- **Organize** – Go through your possessions and let go of anything that does not spark joy.

- **Electronic Vacation** – Take periodic electronic vacations and see how you feel. Leave your phone at home and explore the world around you.

- **Release Unnecessary Worry** – Make a list of what little things get to you so you can bring more awareness to those situations when they arise.

- **Release Perfectionism** – Make a list of what areas of your life you tend to be overly perfectionistic in. Bring awareness to this tendency when it happens and allow your best to be good enough.

PART 4 - YOUR TRANSFORMATION

- **Where Are You Ready to Grow?** – Find out where you have the most room for improvement in your life through taking the survey on page 196.

- **Goal Setting** – Write goals based on where you have the most room for growth.

- **Affirmations** – Create affirmations to align with your most important goals.

- **Commitment Letter** – Write a letter of commitment to yourself about your most important goal.

- **Visualize your future** – Write a story about your ideal future in as much detail as possible.

Appendix B
Resource Guide

Below is a list of some of my most treasured books that relate to the topics discussed in *Empowering the Sensitive Soul*. Each book is open, honest, and inspirational.

1. *Don't Sweat the Small Stuff* – Richard Carlson
2. *Food Rules* – Michael Pollan
3. *Loving What Is* – Byron Katie
4. *Relax and Renew* – Judith Hansen Lasater
5. *The Highly Sensitive Person* – Elaine Aron
6. *The Life Changing Magic of Tidying Up* – Marie Kondo
7. *The Miracle of Mindfulness* – Thich Nhat Hanh
8. *The Power of Now* – Eckhart Tolle
9. *The Slow Down Diet* – Marc David
10. *You Can Heal Your Life* – Louise Hay

Work With Me

It is my personal mission to help other sensitive souls overcome their limiting beliefs and become empowered, strong, and confident in who they are. If you are interested in professional support, I invite you to work with me one-on-one. I will help you sort through the places in your life where you are ready to grow and support you each step of the way on the journey toward healthy and empowered living. I work over the phone and Skype so location is not a limiting factor.

Email: info@christierosen.com
Website: www.christierosen.com
Facebook Group: Empowering the Sensitive Soul
Instagram: christierosen

Spread the Love

If you enjoyed this book, please spread the love by leaving a review on Amazon and/or sharing the book with your friends and family.

Your support means the world to me!

Acknowledgements

My most heartfelt thank you to my family, friends, teachers, and those who have helped me create the book of my dreams, especially:

Eric Gebauer

Carol Wood

Robert Rosen

Jonathan Rosen

Pattie & Peter Gebauer

Helen Sullivan

Carabeth Connolly

Meghan O'Malley

Hanneke Antonelli

Julie Blume

Thomas Hall

Annie Gerrard

Kathrin Lee

Jessica Dalziel

Bobby O'Brien

Ellen Tadd

Gary K. Wolf

Amanda Filippelli

Amie Olson

Marc David

Barbara Benagh

Judith Hanson Lasater

Dr. Richard Delany

Lindsey Smith

Dennis Breyt

Notes

Aron, Elaine. *The Highly Sensitive Person: How to Thrive When the World Overwhelms You*. New York: Broadway, 1997. Print.

Aron, Elaine N. "The Highly Sensitive Person." *The Highly Sensitive Person*. N.p., n.d. Web. 25 Aug. 2016.

Bertolucci, Domonique. Your Best Life: *The Ultimate Guide to Creating the Life You Want*. Sydney: Hodder, 2006. Print.

David, Marc. "The Metabolic Power of Quality." *Psychology of Eating*. N.p., 2014. Web.

David, Marc. *The Slow Down Diet: Eating for Pleasure, Energy, and Weight Loss*. Rochester, VT: Healing Arts, 2005. Print.

David, Marc. "When You Eat Is as Important as What You Eat." *Psychology of Eating*. N.p., 2014. Web.

Dooley, Mike. *Leveraging the Universe: 7 Steps to Engaging Life's Magic*. New York: Atria, 2011. Print.

"EWG's Guide to Safe Drinking Water." *EWG*. Environmental Working Group, n.d. Web.

"EWG's Shopper's Guide to Pesticides in Produce." *Summary*. Environmental Working Group, n.d. Web. 01 Aug. 2016. Web.

"Five Reasons Why You Should Probably Stop Using Antibacterial Soap." *Smithsonian*. N.p., 3 Jan. 2014. Web.

Germer, Christopher K. *The Mindful Path to Self-compassion: Freeing Yourself from Destructive Thoughts and Emotions.* New York: Guilford, 2009. Print.

Hanh, Nhât, and Mai Vo-Dinh. *The Miracle of Mindfulness: A Manual on Meditation.* Boston: Beacon, 1987. Print.

Hay, Louise L. *You Can Heal Your Life.* Bath: Camden, 2008. Print.

Hendricks, Gay. *The Big Leap: Conquer Your Hidden Fear and Take Life to the next Level.* New York, NY: HarperCollins, 2009. Print.

Hyman, Mark. *The UltraMind Solution: Fix Your Broken Brain by Healing Your Body First: The Simple Way to Defeat Depression, Overcome Anxiety and Sharpen Your Mind.* New York: Scribner, 2008. Print.

Katie, Byron, and Stephen Mitchell. *Loving What Is: Four Questions That Can Change Your Life.* New York: Harmony, 2002. Print.

Kondo, Marie. *Life-Changing Magic:* Spark Joy Every Day. N.p.: Random House, 2015. Print.

Lasater, Judith. *Relax and Renew: Restful Yoga for Stressful times.* Berkeley, CA: Rodmell, 1995. Print.

Littlehales, Nick. "How to Supercharge Your Sleep with Nick Littlehales, Sleep Coach to the World's Best Athletes." Audio blog post. *Becoming a Superhuman.com.* N.p., 29 Sept. 2015. Web.

Meindl, Susan. "Highly Sensitive People and Depression." *Highly Sensitive and Creative*. N.p., n.d. Web.

Mercola, Joseph, Dr. "Recent Study Reveals the Effects of Not Drinking Enough Water." *Mercola.com*. N.p., 29 June 2015. Web.

Mercola, Joseph. "New Study Finds Major Toxins in Many Cosmetics." *Mercola.com*. N.p., 4 June 2011. Web.

Ober, Clinton, Stephen T. Sinatra, and Martin Zucker. *Earthing: The Most Important Health Discovery Ever?* Laguna Beach, CA: Basic Health Publications, 2010. Print.

"Organic Agriculture." *U.S. Department of Agriculture*. N.p., June 2016. Web.

Pollan, Michael. *Food Rules: An Eater's Manual*. New York: Penguin, 2009. Print.

"The Pomodoro Technique® - Proudly Developed by Francesco Cirillo." *The Pomodoro Technique®*. N.p., n.d. Web.

"Stress Effects." *The American Institute of Stress*. N.p., n.d. Web.

Tolle, Eckhart. *The Power of Now: A Guide to Spiritual Enlightenment*. Novato, CA: New World Library, 1999. Print.